Hyping the Holocaust:
Scholars Answer Goldhagen

Hyping the Holocaust
Scholars Answer Goldhagen

Franklin H. Littell
Editor

Merion Westfield Press International

This is a project of the

**Philadelphia Center on the
Holocaust, Genocide and Human Rights**

Post Office Box 10
Merion Station, Pennsylvania 19066
Telephone 610/667-5437
FAX 610/667-0265

Made possible by a grant from

The Gutman/Lightner Publication Fund

Second Printing

Printed in the United States of America by:
Merion Westfield Press International
Post Office Box 10
Merion Station, Pennsylvania 19066

For more information or purchases of this or other titles call or FAX:
(610) 667-5437 (voice)
(610) 667-0265 (FAX)

Cover designed, text designed and typeset by:
Cummings & Hathaway Publishers
422 Atlantic Avenue
East Rockaway, New York 11518
1-800-344-7579

Table of Contents

Contributors

Editor *Franklin H. Littell* is Professor (Em.), Temple University (Philadelphia) and Distinguished Visiting Professor, Richard Stockton College of New Jersey

Yehuda Bauer is Emeritus Professor, Hebrew University, and Director of the Research Institute at Yad Vashem, Jerusalem (Israel)

G. Jan Colijn is Dean and Professor of Political Science, Richard Stockton College of New Jersey

Erich Geldbach is Professor of Ecumenical Studies in the Ruhr University, Bochum (Germany)

Wolfgang Gerlach is Senior Pastor in Essen, Germany

Herbert Hirsch is Professor of Political Science, Virginia Commonwealth University (Richmond)

Peter Hoffmann is Professor of History, McGill University, Montreal (Canada)

Eberhard Jäckel is Professor of Modern History, the University of Stuttgart (Germany)

Hubert G. Locke is Professor of Public Service, University of Washington, Seattle

Hans Mommsen is Professor of Modern History in the Ruhr University, Bochum (Germany)

Jacob Neusner is Professor of Religious Studies at the University of South Florida (Tampa) and at Bard College (Annandale, NY)

Richard Pierard is Professor of History, Indiana State University (Terre Haute)

Didier Pollefeyt is a Research Fellow in Moral Theology at the Catholic University of Leuven (Belgium)

Roger W. Smith is Professor of Government at the College of William and Mary (Williamsburg, VA)

Introduction

The serious charges against Daniel J. Goldhagen's book are aroused by its claim to be a scholarly work, subject to appraisal according to the standards of the profession of scholars. *If* the book had been released as a "tract for the times," the responses would not be as hard to categorize as the book itself. Some reviews have been disciplined to accord it the courtesy of an earnest refutation. Others respond to the spirit the book exudes. *If* the book were admittedly a "tract for the times," there still would have been some irritation at lack of accuracy in the use of sources. There would have been some surprise at the dismissive arrogance displayed toward the life work of more mature and careful researchers. Above all there would have remained astonishment that a polemic by a virtually unknown author should be loosed on the public with the Hollywood hype of "Jurassic Park" or a metaphorical "High Noon."

What we have in *Hitler's Willing Executioners* is a diatribe in academic format. We are confronted by "virtual reality." In the spell that is cast "to tell a truth" without too much regard for fairness, critical appraisal or the comparative method, respect for the scientific method is sacrificed to achieve the indictment of a whole people. The show of learning is still there, but "the cognitive model" is shaped by a single passion.

For example, through sleight of hand the statistics are tilted to "prove" the writer's purpose. We may read that "the number of people who were perpetrators is unknown" (p. 11). However, this becoming burst of caution does not last. As to the number of the "willing executioners," as Professor Locke points out in his essay, the total given to suit the writer's purpose in the instant case may be "tens of thousands" (pp. 4, 24), "hundreds of thousands" (pp. 8, 166), "certainly over 100,000" (p. 167), "500,000 or more" (p. 167), "might run into millions" (p. 167).

Even more troubling is the way "the Germans" appears like a drum beat on virtually every page — like the reiterative "the Jews" in a printed antisemitic assault. "The Germans" slides and elides with "the SS," "the Nazis," "ordinary Germans," "Hitler" and "the Nazi leadership" — depending upon the fervor of the moment.

This is not the scientific method at work: it is pamphleteering. A response by concerned scholars has to have an eye to the public reception accorded the book. In the academic world, among Holocaust scholars and historians, there is a consensus: *Hitler's Willing Executioners* is a bad book, prejudiced and repetitious. Academe has already shown it can take care of itself. The public effect of the book, propelled into "bestseller" standing in several countries, is another matter. The exploitation of selected portions of the historical record to undergird a distorted view of "*the* Germans" is wrong, morally, academically and politically.

The scholars who contribute to the present volume do so with a sense of involvement as citizens, of *engagement,* as persons of whom the story and the lessons of the Holocaust today require vigorous action to repair damage to relations between Christians and Jews, between Germans and Israelis and other nations.

Drs. Pollefeyt and Colijn point up the danger in Goldhagen's lack of attention to the comparative dimension of the scientific method. Some members of other national and ethnic blocs, complicit like the Germans in the destruction of Jewish victims, are let home free. The need for every people to reflect upon its role during the Holocaust is thus aborted.

Similarly, Goldhagen's inability to distinguish between the various levels and types of antisemitism lends confusion rather than enlightenment. At ground level, he makes no distinction between Christians and other gentiles. Yet at least since the time of the French Revolution that line of distinction has been as discernable in "the Christian world" as the line between the observant and the anti-clerical in "the Jewish world."

His writing swings recklessly between theological antisemitism, cultural antisemitism, and modern political antisemitism. He obviously cannot make the imperative distinctions, and he therefore sweepingly condemns "Christians" (aka gentiles) without understanding the problematic of "Christendom." The tragedy of the Church Struggle *(Kirchenkampf)* escapes him entirely, and again it is "*the* Germans" who are found guilty. The rest of "Christendom" is let home free.

A scholarly masterpiece may last for generations; as Professor Bauer here says, Goldhagen's book will not go in the Pantheon. But a "tract for the times" must be judged according to the times in which it appears. According to the printed date, *Hitler's Willing Executioners* appeared in 1996. Its real spiritual and intellectual date is 1945. A half century later, when the Holocaust — the genocide of the Jews by the dictatorship of the "Third Reich" — is remembered and discussed, sensitivity and a low tone of voice are preferable to arrogance and self-righteousness.

Even "the Germans" have earned the right to be treated fairly today

— not to mention senior scholars who have spent decades in fighting study of the Holocaust through the political and intellectual establishments, long before any young writer or eager publisher could capitalize on the brute fact that today "there's no business like Shoah business."

Franklin H. Littell

· Chapter 1 ·

Leaving Evil in Germany: The Questionable Success of Goldhagen in the Low Countries

Didier Pollefeyt and G. Jan Colijn

· 1 ·

Leaving Evil in Germany:
The Questionable Success of Goldhagen
in the Low Countries

Didier Pollefeyt and G. Jan Colijn

While a number of standard works about Nazi genocide, including Hilberg's *Destruction of European Jews*, have never been translated into Dutch, the translation of *Hitler's Willing Executioners*[1] was rushed to the market in May 1996. Nicely packaged and translated, the book was recommended in a well-publicized, broad[2] Dutch and Belgian advertising campaign as "controversial" and "shocking" because "it will fundamentally change the vision on the Holocaust and on Germany in the Nazi era." Meanwhile the book has been among the top ten bestsellers in the Netherlands and Flanders (Belgium's Dutch language region) for months.

Although the Dutch translation preceded the German and French translation,[3] a vehement controversy had already erupted in Germany with articles in *Der Spiegel* and *Die Zeit*. In all likelihood it was this controversy in particular that contributed to the wide attention which the Dutch translation got in virtually all prominent Dutch and Belgian papers and periodicals. For purposes of this study we analyzed thirty five reviews, the overwhelming majority of those available in serious papers and periodicals by the summer of 1996. As always, some scholarly analyses will emerge later in the literature. Goldhagen's book is placed within the context of the "new controversy" in almost all reviews. "An American study, of which the German translation is not even ready yet, has created a storm in the Bundesrepublik which is already viewed by Die Zeit as a new phase in the 'Historikerstreit'," stated the Dutch paper *Het Parool*.[4]

Generally, the leading Dutch language reviewers of Goldhagen's work are rather matter-of-fact. They recognize and regret the anti-Germanism of Goldhagen as well as the anti-Americanism of some of his (German) critics, subsequently reduce the pretended scientific value of this book to its real proportions, and then subject the study to businesslike, but un-yielding scientific criticisms. Finally the fascinating question arises ex-actly why this book has raised so much dust and has become a bestseller in the Netherlands and in Belgium.

Beyond anti-Germanism and anti-Americanism

Dutch language reviews clearly warn about the anti-German tone of Goldhagen's book. For example, Willem Beusekamp writes in the Dutch *de Volkskrant* that "the American (has) such a crashing dislike of Ger-mans" that he devised the following thesis:

> All Germans are antisemites and have passionately been longing for the extermination of Jews for centuries.
> Hitler came as if sent for. Afterwards Goldhagen amassed the material to support his thesis scientifically.[5]

In the same paper, German sociologist Peter Glotz wrote that "... the Americans appear to believe that fifty years of democracy have had no effect whatsoever on the Germans."[6] In the authoritative Belgian paper *De Standaard* the historian Georgi Verbeeck echoes Beusekamp's notion that the book will rekindle anti-German feelings above all: "Goldhagen's book will certainly be enthusiastically received by the small army of ad-mirers that does not tire to proclaim that Germany shall have to 'cope' with new revelations about itself."[7] Goldhagen's hostile tone with respect to current Germany is not well received among most reviewers. "The notion that the country avoids an honest confrontation with its own past sounds, of course, convincing to someone who does not know the pertinent impressive and historical debates in Germany."[8] Dutch colum-nist Jan Blokker notes that it is a red herring to point an accusatory finger at Germany after fifty years of conscious *Bewältigung* with the past. Blokker also notes that most German commentators question why Germans need to be berated about matters they already know by an American "junior" who has very little experience in the Holocaust field.[9]

Dutch-speaking reviewers also target the anti-American reactions among German commentators. Boevink characterizes critics, from those of the *Frankfurter Allgemeine Zeitung* to the *Tagezeitung*, as a bunch of wild dogs tearing at Goldhagen's provocations, and he singles out the critique of Goldhagen in the *Frankfurter Allgemeine* as unvarnished anti-

Americanism.[10] Along similar lines Verbeeck writes that

> ... not all criticism which Goldhagen had to endure in the Ameri-
> can and German press (is) just. It is, for example, unnecessary to
> point to his Jewish ancestry and to the role of his father, Erich
> Goldhagen ... Some critics have too easily used the escape that
> 'everything is already known.'
> Goldhagen has rightly asked attention for the nameless execu-
> tioners of the genocide.[11]

The scientific contribution of Goldhagen reduced to its true proportions

Contrary to the heated debates in Germany and the United States it can
be said that Dutch commentators display a remarkably sober attitude
toward the publication. Its scientific value is questioned. The historian
von der Dunk notes that, whereas Goldhagen cleverly and systematically
constructs an indictment for a tribunal, the book is of no value to historians. There are no new, previously unknown facts. Von der Dunk criti-
cizes Goldhagen's "distorted depiction" of Holocaust literature to under-
line his own originality and he finds especially steep Goldhagen's contention that he is in fact the first one to focus on ordinary executioners.[12]
Verbeeck is surprised by the media attention and by the emotional reactions about the book especially as Goldhagen "unashamedly kicks in open
doors and appears to by-pass years of historiographical and political-
ideological discussion."[13] Bas Blokker's critique of Goldhagen's pretense
to be original could not agree more with the position of Verbeeck. "Anyone who has even slightly followed the historical debate about the destruction of the Jews cannot be surprised, and certainly not shocked about
the content of this book."[14]

To a certain degree, Goldhagen has triggered some of the sharp reactions in Germany himself. Johannes Houwink Ten Cate argues in *de
Volkskrant* that Goldhagen allowed his critics several openings, with his
"unlimited ambition," his "boundless pretension" and the "denigrating
characterizations" of German intellectuals who have written on the Holocaust.[15] Verbeeck takes umbrage with the "caricature" of the historiographical tradition in Goldhagen's work especially when he then proudly de-
fends his "... pretended 'new' insights."[16] And the Dutch press echoes similar
views. Friso Wielenga argues in *Vrij Nederland* that it is "... scientifically
not becoming to present much longer known data as new facts."[17] Wielenga

qualifies this critique by noting that if Goldhagen would have simply used the undeveloped source materials with which he works to indicate that the circles of those involved in the Holocaust were larger than previously thought, he would have become less well known but he would have been taken more seriously by colleagues.[18] "For Goldhagen this more modest goal was obviously insufficient and that is regrettable because most of the attention is now claimed by his untenable conclusions.[19]

Goldhagen, "not hampered by modesty"[20] places himself partially beside, partially above European history and the historiography about the Holocaust. However, most Dutch language commentators in the low countries situate his work firmly within the framework of existing, solid traditional research, and question and qualify his book within that context. The conclusions of the important reviewers are then fairly similar. Verbeeck notes that the book is "... certainly not worth a second *Historikerstreit*."[21] And von der Dunk agrees that, if the expectation of a new *Historikerstreit* will come true, it will be "... a very superfluous fight.[22] In the next several sections we detail some of the specific points in Goldhagen's work that have been subject to fairly unanimous criticism.

Straight ahead to untenable conclusions (Friso Wielenga)

Von der Dunk notes that, irrespective of the depth of other disagreements, there is a consensus among experts everywhere "... that monocausal explanations and a determinist vision on the Shoah and the Third Reich are inadequate."[23] Bert van Oosterhout notes in the Dutch *Algemeen Dagblad:* "The methodological criticism of Goldhagen's work centers around his attempt to reduce the whole judeocide to one cause and that means that the scientific clock is turned back."[24] Friso Wielenga writes that Goldhagen breaks with a penchant in history for "multicausal" explanations of the Holocaust. Goldhagen's "monocausal" approach feeds "... the need for simple and linear explanations."[25] Bert van Oosterhout accuses Goldhagen of ignoring all material that does not fit his thesis,[26] and the Belgian periodical *Knack* notes a tendency toward "monomania".[27] *Knack's* historian, Marc Reynebeau, continues:

> Goldhagen, in his book as well as in interviews, continually calls on his critics to provide evidence that he is wrong. Such behavior is not quite correct; according to the falsification method it is up to the author himself to refine his hypotheses by seeking for arguments which contradict them.[28]

Consensus about this point is virtually unanimous. Wielenga notes in *Vrij Nederland:*

> Goldhagen pushes all these [counterarguments] arrogantly to the side and puts his own monocausal explanation against them: *the* Germans were the willing executioners in the murder of millions because they were obsessed with a 'demonic antisemitism of the virulent racial variety.'[29]

Von der Dunk even points out that Goldhagen's linear explanation of the origin of this evil mirrors the Nazi explanation in that his a-historical monocausal determinism (*"the* Germans") is an inverted portent of racist conceptualization.[30] A similar notion is found in the work of Belgian Holocaust specialist v-an den Berghe.

> There is no doubt that Hitler and his acolytes considered judeo-bolshevism such a quadrated, monocausal evil, that [they] were consequently convinced they could eliminate all evil from this world by destroying this singular cause.[31]

German antisemitism: the elimination of a monocausal hypothesis

The central point here is made by Verbeeck:

> Goldhagen's vision about the 'exceptional' character of antisemitism in Germany, that inevitably was to end in the extermination of the Jews, is utterly problematic... Herewith Goldhagen goes against the growing historical insight that modern antisemitism is not a uniquely 'German' phenomenon and that it is insufficient breeding ground for persecution and extermination. The existence of an antisemitic tradition is — of course — not called into question by this, it is only not considered a decisive factor.[32]

This citation typifies most criticisms of Goldhagen. On the one hand the critics point to the fact that antisemitism was a necessary but certainly insufficient condition for the realization of the Holocaust. On the other it is noted that antisemitism is not a specifically German but a much more broadly spread circumstance.

With regard to the first point it is repeatedly brought up that the propagated April 1, 1933 boycott of Jewish shops in Germany was not a success and that the *Reichskristallnacht* garnished by no means the massive support that the regime had intended.[33] Moreover, several moments in *Third Reich* history clearly indicate that the Nazi regime did not succeed in turning latent antisemitism among the population into murderous pogroms. Van Oosterhout notes:

> Germans generally did not react with enthusiasm to the gradual radicalization of the persecution of Jews after *Kristallnacht*. After the first German defeat criticism about the antisemitic policy of the Nazis increased, even if it was only through feelings of guilt or fear. Goldhagen does not breathe a word of it.[34]

Dutch researchers Rüter and Dick advance the argument "... that vulgar opportunism has more explanatory value than antisemitism, in relation to the question why many Germans in the Third Reich cooperated with genocide."[35] Apart from this point, the reviews systematically qualify antisemitism as a phenomenon. Wielenga, for example, notes the need to make distinctions among many forms of more or less explicit racism, from implicit antisemitic sentiments to murdering Jews with sadistic pleasure, and warns that if such distinctions are not made, "... cowardly and indifferent observation of the social ghettoization of Jews in the thirties is not only put on par with (secret) support of this policy, but also with murder itself."[36]

With regard to the second point, made above — the reference to the ubiquitous nature of European antisemitism — antisemitism is understood to exist in a broader context. The paper *De Morgen* asks: "Why did Goldhagen not research the motives of the Poles, Ukrainians and other people who participated in the persecution of Jews?"[37] Particularly striking is that commentators search their own heart in relation to European antisemitism. Van Oosterhout notes in the Dutch *Algemeen Dagblad* that Goldhagen passed over "... antisemitism in France, the pogroms in eastern Europe and numerous other manifestations of hatred of Jews, *including those in the Netherlands*[38] (italics added). Von der Dunk notes that the allies did not bomb the railroads or the camps. He also discusses the passivity of the population in occupied countries and their occasional collaboration in the deportation of Jews and he muses that the principal distinction between a German railroad man involved in the transport of Jews and his Dutch or French counterpoint is his German passport.[39] The Belgian periodical *Knack* is even more to the point. It recalls that during the thirties it was possible in Belgium to issue public calls for discrimination against Jews. It recalls that Einstein was banned from delivering a peace message at the pre-war *Ijzerbedevaart* (a pro-Flemish pilgrimage) because he was a Jew, and *Knack* points out that current Dutch usage continues to contain biased views about Jewry. These examples support the notion that the presumed uniqueness of German antisemitism deserves qualification.[40] Van den Berghe notes that the United States is not blameless either:

> Just ten days after the *Anschluss* the United States proposed an international conference to regulate the emigration of German and Austrian Jews to the free world. In expectation of that conference nothing constructively happened. Borders remained hermetically closed, the line of those waiting in front of the embassies in Germany and Austria continued to grow.[41]

There is, as Auschwitz survivor Arnoni wrote "... something more tragic than the Holocaust: the nonchalance, the tepidity with which humanity as a whole has swallowed the Holocaust, made light of it, walked a big arc around it, has rendered itself immune from it."[42]

Collective guilt

In an interview with the Dutch *de Volkskrant* Goldhagen denied vehemently that his theses can be interpreted as proof that the Germans are collectively guilty:

> Sure, I generalize by consistently talking about 'the Germans.' That is a very normal way of generalizing which decidedly does no violence to the truth. Americans in the south used to be racists who called blacks niggers and considered them inferior. Nobody wants to challenge that either.[43]

Commentators in the low countries do not agree. Verbeeck contends that Goldhagen may deny any accusation of collective guilt but that such an accusation is submerged in his "generalizing approach to German responsibility."[44] Reynebeau states: "What is disconcerting in Goldhagen's conclusion is that he answers the question of guilt by pointing the finger to the German people as a whole in a unmistakably inquisitorial tone."[45]

Wielenga writes that while Goldhagen does not use the term collec-

tive guilt and has claimed since the publication of the book that he did
not intend to raise collective guilt, the book *is* permeated with that generalizing thesis. Wielenga adds that Goldhagen "... reduces the discussion to the level in the immediate post-war period and that is meagre for
a scientific product of a half a century later."[46] Reynebeau agrees and
points out that the implicit and strongly moralizing option of collective
guilt has scarcely been defended since the fifties.[47] There was some ad-
herence to the notion of collective guilt immediately after the war, partly
because of understandable revengefulness, partly on scientific grounds,
especially among psychologists in the United States. For instance, the
idea of collective guilt was at the basis of the denazification programs
through which Americans wanted to re-educate the Germans. The late
Willy Brandt, who spent the war in exile, characterized these not very
successful programs as "bureaucratized witch trials." But as early as the
Nuremberg trials the idea of collective guilt was no longer accepted.[48]
Verbeeck notes "... that thesis is not only unjust but, moreover, it does
not recognize a complex historical reality. 'Collective' guilt obscures individual guilt and offers a way out from the differentiation of personal
responsibilities."[49]

In line with these criticisms we can recapitulate that Goldhagen again
threatens to imitate schemes of the Nazis by his notion of collective guilt.
The general point was made by Yehuda Bauer several years ago.[50] To say
that *the* Germans are responsible for the Holocaust is as absurd as to say
that *the* Jews are responsible for the crucifixion of Christ. One has to
judge people for what they are and not on the basis of membership in a
group. The idea of collective guilt was stamped into the Nazis themselves
extremely well. Every Jew was reduced to an element of a well-defined
group which had been found 'guilty' in its totality. This explains why
under the Nazis ten Jews were executed time and again for the flight of
one single Jew. All members of the (Jewish) group are, after all, responsible for the acts of a single Jew.

When Goldhagen slightly modified his contested theses about collective German guilt, the Dutch language press gave considerable attention to the matter. Winfried Dolderer noted in *De Standaard* that according to Goldhagen the image of the "Jew as enemy" now existed among
"many" and no longer among "all Germans." Dolderer added the following *coup de grace*: "If Goldhagen had formulated his thesis this way from
the beginning then he might perhaps have only kicked some open doors
in German knowledge."[51]

The paradox of demonization

Jaap de Berg muses in the Protestant daily *Trouw* that Goldhagen gives the impression that Germany has for centuries consisted of just two kinds of people, antisemites and Jews.[52] Friso Wielenga notes in *Vrij Nederland* that Goldhagen violates his own admonition not to make caricatures out of Germans.[53] Marc Reynebeau critiques the central foundation of Goldhagen's book, the notion that antisemitism in Germany had developed to the point that it had become part of the national character. Reynebeau questions whether one can ascribe as self-evident such an "... eternal and unalienable character or national trait", and he also asserts that it is very difficult to gauge correctly the representativeness of opinions and apparently self-evident characteristics in a context of war, censorship and propaganda.[54]

Rüter and Dick contend that Goldhagen has succumbed to the temptation to demonize the Germans.[55] Van den Berghe describes demonization as the "... intentionalization of all acts of the opponent while rendering absolute his power to realize what he pursues. To the enemy is ascribed the malice and omnipotence of the devil, the counterpart of divine providence."[56] Criticism of demonization is well-known. The distance between perpetrators and victims, between them and us, becomes insurmountable. The lesson to be drawn from an atrocity, that civilized people are capable of atrocities, is turned upside down: only Germans commit these atrocities. Demonization turns our eyes away from reality, as van den Berghe argues.[57] Von der Dunk gave the same warning to Dutch readers:

> Can we suffice by saying: those were the Germans. That will not happen to us. Or do we have to say: Germans are people like us and so we have to be mindful of evil? These are difficult questions with which we are rather not confronted, all the more when we appear to live in a world wherein daily atrocities happen. Think of Rwanda. Think of Bosnia. We rather look the other way and say: evil, that was then, that was the Germans, or if need be the Nazis, but fortunately that nightmare is behind us. Because of the human tendency to see evil foremost outside of ourselves, it is sensible to read again, next to Goldhagen's *Hitler's Willing Executioners*, the essay that Hannah Arendt wrote briefly after the Eichmann trial.[58]

Finally, several reviews point out that such a demonization of the

Germans runs aground in a paradox. Henri Beunders summarizes the problem as follows:

> If the German people were predestined to the Holocaust, that fact will not enlarge German guilt, but rather diminish it. For a feeble-minded criminal is "not competent" and therefore not personally responsible.[59]

Demonization indeed implies something "deterministic."[60] When Germans are simply enacting their devilish national character, then the moral meaning of the genocide is of the same magnitude as an earthquake. As Dijkhuis argues: "... an irritating consequence of Goldhagen's thesis is that the personal responsibility of nazi crimes disappears from sight: he renders an entire people not competent through the deeply rooted antisemitic obsession."[61] On this point too there is unanimity in the reviews. Reynebeau writes in the Belgian weekly *Knack:*

> If what Goldhagen states adds up, [the Germans] did not do more than their social duty. For in his theory the executioners were blinded by racist bias. They had been bestowed with this from childhood. They can not possibly assume full, undivided personal responsibility. For as a result of permanent and therefore, according to Goldhagen, obsessive indoctrination they were in fact in a state of lesser competency.[62]

Eight reasons for Goldhagen's success in the low countries

The question arises why Goldhagen's work can draw so much attention in light of sharp and rather unanimous criticisms in the Dutch language reviews. For despite all criticisms the book is an undeniable sales success. Several commentators wonder about the broad public interest in the study. Von der Dunk notes: "What is remarkable is not the book but the fuss that is made over it. Contentious works are regularly published without all media eagerly swooping down on [them]."[63] Jaap Tanja contends in the *Nederlands Israëlitisch Weekblad* that "... the discussion about and resulting from this scientific study, written with remarkable anger and indignation, [is] more interesting than the book itself."[64]

From the Dutch language reviews we can distil eight reasons for the success of *Hitlers Gewillige Beulen*. These reasons must be situated within the context of the warnings that the commentators issue against

Goldhagen's slanted positions, positions which undoubtedly exercise power of attraction over the Dutch language readers, i.e. the monocausal explanation, typically German antisemitism, the collective guilt hypothesis and the demonization of the perpetrators.

Above all, of course, there is fascination with the subject — the extreme evil of the Holocaust. Public interest feeds on the universal symbolism of the Holocaust as a negative myth, to use Margalit and Motzkin's apt phrase, that infuses Western culture "... with a certain degree of nihilism, for it contains an intuition as to how fragile and tentative our culture is."[65] Von der Dunk adds:

> And of course we are dealing with the theme that will always strike allergic chords as such. The most perfect incarnation of evil and of moral perversion singularly escapes pure scientific historiography and a definitive explanation.[66]

And Wielenga adds in turn: "Perhaps the explanation for this disproportionate attention rests with the enduring fascination with the evil of the millionfold murder."[67] Supplementing such fascination is Goldhagen's monocausal approach. Again, Wielenga: "His simple and linear explanation of Evil is possibly also an attractive aspect."[68] The genesis of the Holocaust is reduced, in final analysis, to one, over-arching, monocausal factor: antisemitism. Its theme does not demand a lot of its readers, it is neither complex nor multi-layered. This monocausal thesis is virtually free of cautious qualifiers. At the large international conference *Remembering for the Future II* (Berlin, 1994) the centrality of German antisemitism was reflected in more than two dozen papers on the subject, thirty one if we include papers also focusing on issues of general xenophobia. More differentiated and sophisticated views abounded, with foci on antisemitism elsewhere, or on issues that bring shades of nuance, e.g. the German church struggle; yet the tedium of greater complexity in alternative assessments of the Holocaust is of little interest to a larger audience. Goldhagen wanted to prosecute, shock and provoke — and he succeeded. Bas Blokker notes:

> The historical debate is just not a spectator sport. It is more like chess, two men virtually motionless at a table, completely uninteresting until you absorb yourself in their moves. Goldman [sic] is a chess player who shows up with boxing gloves, gives his opponent an uppercut and stops his clock. Aficionados of the

game are not waiting for this, but he will never again have to complain about lack of public interest.[69]

Prosecutors, more than historians, would concentrate on the elimination of Jews as a German national product, and test the hypothesis by comparing Germany antisemitism with only its Danish and Italian variants. No prosecutor would risk a comparison with France. Keep it simple.

A third reason for Goldhagen's success is that popular culture is intentionalist and demonizing. Demonization addresses the profound popular need to divide humanity into "us" vs. "them." Popular historiography is dominated to a considerable degree by a tendency to make matters black and white, without nuances or complexities. Primo Levi has argued that the stream of human events is reduced in popular tradition to conflicts and conflicts to duels: "us" and "them," "Athenians and Spartans," "Romans and Carthaginians." The popularity of Goldhagen's book can be compared with the enormous current popularity of spectator sports where two teams face each other, clearly distinguishable and recognizable, and where, at the end of the game there are winners and losers with whom the individual can identify. Levi argues that those who study the Holocaust have the same need to separate good from evil, to choose sides as if rendering the last judgment.[70] Human differentiation and complexity in relation to good and evil are indeed reduced by Goldhagen to a fascinating confrontation between what Finkielkraut called "Innocence" and the "Repulsive Monster."[71] Intentionalism reduces the complex extermination process that developed during several years along similar lines to one single cause: the intention of one or several individuals. Through this reduction we can situate in the background of this genocide the operation of an unbelievably monstrous and satanic will. Doing so allows us to localize (and condemn) evil with precision.

In the fourth place it is clear that the book resonates with anti-German attitudes in a number of Western countries, e.g., England, France, Belgium and Netherlands. Those attitudes are not constant and perhaps more *salonfähig* than virulent, but many of Germany's neighbors will have to fight second nature, and sit on their hands instead of breaking into applause after reading Goldhagen's anti-German treatise. Von der Dunk has a particular ear for Dutch sensitivity to anti-German stimuli:

The tendency to see the big neighbor even today as the rapist of 1940-1945 appears not to have disappeared. [And this] in spite of all pragmatic intentions and official-public declarations of

Hyping the Holocaust

recent time that bygones should be bygones and that today's Germany is not that of yesterday. The occupation is still much too much present in our culture [for that].[72]

This point creates perhaps the biggest chasm between more objective scholars and the personally colored anti-German historical consciousness of the average reader in the Low Countries. However, this phenomenon is difficult to trace, even more so to measure. A letter to the editor of *Het Parool* gives us a glimpse of its manifestation. F.L. Meijler, whose parents perished in Auschwitz, writes this about Germans:

> Whenever they go or stand, whichever library they visit, to whatever country they travel, they are eternally doomed to know that no bigger crime has ever been done and that only Germany possessed the technique and degree of organization to execute a scenario such as described here... From the reactions to Goldhagen it is clear that one regrets the Holocaust above all because the world does not stop harping on it. The Holocaust was not carried out by some individuals, but by a perfect organization which, given its size and duration, must have been carried by the whole population.[73]

A fifth reason is that Goldhagen's work resonates strongly with a tendency toward self-righteousness.[74] Homo Hollanditis is indeed a Dutch uncle, especially in international affairs. In the Dutch case, this tendency turns Germany into a "contrast-nation," to borrow von der Dunk's phrase, and fueling this differentiation is the myth of the "good" Dutch in World War II.[75] These interrelated cultural realities create a climate wherein an anti-German book will always sell within this context. Von der Dunk compares the demythologization of certain areas in Dutch history with the Nazi era:

> [What] also plays a role is that we have been reminded through diverse cases especially the past few years that our own past contains chapters which have yet not been digested, e.g., the never officially punished outrages in Indonesia and the maltreatments after 1945 in NSB camps [NSB: Nationaal-Socialistische Beweging — the Dutch Nazis]. But as these sink away to nothingness compared with Nazi atrocities, so our self-criticism sinks away to nothingness compared to the German one.[76]

Scholars Answer Goldhagen

By focusing on the German evil, one can overlook one's own evil from colonial or wartime, and the same holds true for Belgium. The Dutch, and the Belgians, as Henri Beunders puts, like "to leave Evil in Germany."[77] Of course, we may stretch the canvass beyond Germany. Cambodia, Burundi, and Bosnia certainly point to the potential of evil in all of us, but we rather not face it. It is much more comfortable to situate evil beyond our borders, just as it is to think we have nothing in common with Germans. Freud's notion of the narcissism of minor difference, so elegantly resuscitated in Michael Ignatieff's *Blood and Belonging*, is of utility here: reduce the Holocaust to "Made in Germany," and Germany's neighbors are granted precisely that kind of distinction that helps maintain their separate identity and to whitewash their own complicity in the destruction of European Jews. "The evil one is the other", a very Nazi kind of reasoning.

The sixth factor to which repeated attention is drawn in the Low Countries is that the success of the book is related to the moment at which the wound of Germany is again reopened. Journaille writes in *Het Parool*:

> At the very moment that the Fourth Reich wants to enter the new age as the most powerful human nation of the new Europe (previously called Neuropa) one of these American cultural barbarians wanders through their china closet.[78]

Willem Breedveld notes in *Trouw* that the new elements which Goldhagen brings forth are especially inflammatory because they appear at the very moment that "... Kohl's Germany reaches a high point in its political history...."[79] Lambiek Berends echoes this notion. He asserts that Goldhagen touches "a raw nerve among Germans who hoped to have settled with the past after the *Historikerstreit* and above all after reunification".[80] But it is that very reunification that triggers questions about Germany's position in the current European line-up. As Beunders puts the issue: "These Germans were no good, are no good and will never be good. So you better not give them a leading role in Europe."[81]

Wielenga wonders whether "... Goldhagen's continuous reference to the Germans" is coupled with "... the implicit thought that things in Germany are still not what they ought to be."[82] Germany, as strongest central European power, as indispensable catalyst of integration, should lead but not dominate. The memory of its past can be a useful curb in this regard. Germans cannot escape their past and Goldhagen's book plays a role in this. Von der Dunk cynically finds it a "... reassuring thought."[83] But there are repeated warnings against this train of thought. Van Oosterhout notes:

> It would look bad for Germany and Europe if [Goldhagen] was right. For this reason Germany ought not to be allowed another *Alleingang*. Especially after reunification it ought to become embedded in Europe so that historical doubts and frustrations do not raise their head again.[84]

The seventh and eight reason for Goldhagen's success bring us to more fundamental cultural-philosophical considerations. The pulse of late twentieth century capitalism relies on relentless marketing, advertising, often simply on hype. High culture, e.g., the more serious end of the publishing industry, does not escape the prerequisite marketing hype. In a crude, ever coarsening, aggressive culture, Goldhagen's book succeeds because it is masterfully hyped. Von der Dunk states the point as follows:

> We are also dealing with the current uncritical susceptibility to every sensational thesis in scholarship at which advertising takes aim. It does not matter whether it is *right* as long as it is *new*. New! that is the formula for sales success.[85]

As von der Dunk notes: "Historians too, squint with one eye at history, and with the other to the market."[86]

An eighth reason is related to the nature of today's academic research. Another kind of market force plays a role here. Higher education has been a buyers' market for some time, certainly in the liberal arts. Jobs are scarce. Pressures on young scholars to make their mark are tremendous. The publication of one's dissertation is often a prerequisite to get tenure, to get promoted, to get noticed, and, for job searchers, simply to get in. Despite calls for greater emphasis on quality teaching, 'publish or perish' remains a truism for much of higher education, certainly at research universities. As public funding per (student) capita declines everywhere, the institutional pursuit of third stream revenues intensifies, and competition for grants increases. With total research and development funding constant at best, the pressures to produce research *results* are enormous. On occasion these pressures lead to scientific incompetence, even fraud, but at issue here is the relentless pursuit of new results or paradigm shifts *per se*.

The success of Goldhagen's book is undoubtedly related to his publisher's relentless hype. It is that hype which made Goldhagen's book a bestseller, unlike, for example, John Weiss' *Ideology of Death* published earlier this year which asks the same questions and comes to virtually similar but more nuanced conclusions. However, Goldhagen's work also arises in a climate of unrelenting pressure on researchers to produce results, new results, and to publish those results fast — to produce to get grants, and to get grants to produce some more. Postmodernism allows the social sciences arguably a greater latitude to leap to new truths than would be possible and permissible in the natural sciences. Goldhagen's book reflects a shrewd understanding of these realities, and of the opportunities for would-be iconoclasts[87] in our popular culture: the chance to repackage conclusions reached earlier in the relatively hidden scholarly confines of any academic field in a new, provocative way. In a recent *New Yorker* essay on popular culture, David Denby laments the current *Zeitgeist* as full of derision, "... the spirit of the jammed, crazy, relentless talk, the needling spirits of radio, of late night TV."[88]

Goldhagen's book is a paragon of such derision. Any exegesis at odds with his own is dismissed, as incomplete, insufficient, unsatisfactory, wrongheaded or, perhaps, inopportune. Combined with the exhaustive array of examples on the horror of the Holocaust this derisive sweep of contending treatments is meant to shift paradigms in current thinking about the Holocaust, and culminates in one simple and popular trouvaille: it was the Huns, Jack.

The relentless search for new paradigms is an industrial reality in, especially, the academic world. Goldhagen managed to convince his dissertation committee and others (including the American Political Science Association which granted his dissertation, the basis for his book, the Galbriel A. Almond Award for the best in comparative [sic] politics) that he had found a new paradigm. The imperative of new paradigms was wedded to a remarkably successful marketing campaign which shrewdly grafted its hype onto deep pre-existing resentments and biases in Europe and also in the United States.[89] The ultimate consequence of *Hitler's Willing Executioners* and its surrounding publicity is — and this is a consequence that cannot make Goldhagen comfortable — that the whole episode gives credence to the crude cynicism that there is no business like Shoah business.

· Chapter 2 ·

The Goldhagen Fallacy

Hubert Locke

· 2 ·

The Goldhagen Fallacy

Hubert Locke

David Goldhagen's *Hitler's Willing Executioners* is undoubtedly one of the most sweeping polemics to be published in recent years. It scorns much of a half-century of painstaking research and study on the destruction of European Jewry during the era of the German Third Reich. It dismisses the careful findings, the informed judgments and the considered opinions of several generations of eminent scholars, many of whom have devoted a lifetime to inquiry on the monumental horror of the twentieth century. It denounces, often at considerable length, interpretations it deems "deficient" [p. 8], "marred by a poor understanding and an under-theorizing" [p. 7] or marked by "grave error" [p. 14]. The presumptuousness of such a massive rejection of nearly everything that preceded it is enough to give one considerable pause. If, however, we take the book at face value, what does it have to offer?

Hitler's Willing Executioners rests on the conviction that six million European Jewish citizens were murdered because of an innate and unique mindset that is peculiar to the German people. "The men and women who in some intimate way knowingly contributed to the slaughter of Jews," Goldhagen writes, "were overwhelmingly and most importantly Germans" [p. 6]. The murder of the Jews was an effort uniquely German "because what can be said about the Germans cannot be said about any other nationality or about all of the nationalities combined" [p. 6]. The participation of Germans in the Jewish genocide was not merely that of committed Nazis; "an enormous number of ordinary Germans ... who had no particular affiliation with Nazi institutions like the Party or the SS provided personnel for the camp system" [p. 177-178]. Evidence of the capacity of ordinary Germans to murder Jews can be further seen in the operations of the Order Police, "a group less Nazified than average for German society [p. 185] ... but "broadly representative of German society" [p. 277] which "easily [became] genocidal killers" [p. 185]. Thus, "while Germans should not be caricatured" [p. 382] antisemitism is "a pathology afflicting all Germans" [p. 387] and "the conclusions drawn about the overall character of the [Police Battalion] can indeed must be, generalized *to the German people in general"* [p. 402].

How seriously should one take such a sweeping indictment of an entire nation of people? For most readers, it will depend on the amount and quality of the evidence presented and the persuasiveness of the arguments advanced. In this case, both argument and evidence suffer from what is an unfortunate tendency toward bombast, combined with a highly selective use of the reams of material available to scholars on the era.

A.

A primary problem which appears throughout the book is depicted in a brief discussion of the infamous economic boycott of 1 April 1933. The boycott is recounted as "a signal event" in the early months of National Socialist rule and the question is raised: how did Germans react to the boycott? After acknowledging that "one Jew recounts that a few Germans defiantly expressed their solidarity with the beleaguered Jews", Goldhagen asserts that "the general attitude of the public" was reflected in an incident also cited by a lone Jewish observer who tells of a German woman, accompanied by two uniformed Nazis, who returned goods purchased earlier to a chemist because she didn't know the chemist was a Jew.

We have, in the first instance, a claim about the general attitude of the German populace based on the testimony of one observer citing a single incident. Much of the evidence cited in this work is similarly anecdotal. For many, such testimony is far from decisive. More important, however, is the fact that there is another side to the story of the 1933 boycott. There is a considerable body of testimony which indicates that the boycott was initially planned for a full week but, for several reasons, ended up being limited to one day or called off earlier than planned because it did not engender public support.[1] For Goldhagen, however, the boycott was a display of "the German Volk ... "collectively boycotting an entire group of German citizens" in a "large-scale assault" which was ... "devastating to the social position of the Jews."[2]

When one moves beyond these general considerations, we find the following issues.

On Methodology

Some of the most important contributions to scholarship in the social sciences have been found in the methodological appendices to classic social science texts. Gunnar Myrdal's monumental study of race in the United States,[3] for example, has been generally hailed not only for its path-breaking insights but also the astuteness of its methodological approach to this intractable issue. Thus, in a work like *Hitler's Willing Executioners*, which makes such huge and categoric declarations, one wants to pay especial attention to the approach its author has taken to the materials he uses in framing his study, and to the way in which its author has gone about the task of marshalling and mounting his arguments and evidence.

Hitler's Willing Executioners also has a methodological appendix. From it, we learn that:

a. the documentary evidence on which the work is based is scant. "A problem in studying the perpetrators is the unevenness of the extant material", states Goldhagen. "Contemporary documents which illuminate in sufficient detail the perpetrators' actions, or anything at all about their motivations, barely exist. About some institutions of killing" [i.e., the police battalions, the work camps, and the death marches] "virtually no contemporary documents of any kind have survived. Therefore, the primary material for this study has been drawn mainly from materials amassed during the Federal Republic of Germany's postwar legal investigations of Nazi crimes".[4]

b. this source, however, on which the thesis of the book is primarily constructed, is in itself questionable. "This rich, illuminating postwar testimony is also a problematic source. [The] testimony [of the perpetrators] is replete with omissions, half-truths, and lies.... Because of this, the only methodological position that makes sense is to discount all self-exculpating testimony that finds no corroboration from other sources."[5]

We are confronted with a work, therefore, whose arguments rest on scanty evidence, much of which is problematic and subject to being discounted because of the questionable character and motives of the informants. In spite of this, however, we are further told that:

c. the three "institutions" ... permit the motivations of the perpetrators in those particular institutions to be uncovered, and also allow for generalizing in those particular institutions to the perpetrators as a group and to ... the German people. Much of what is said here about methods ... pertains both to the perpetrators and to the larger population of Germans."[6]

These are three rather extraordinary assertions! They are sufficient to leave a reader more than a bit doubtful about the soundness of the book and its conclusions. As it turns out, this is only the tip of a huge problematic iceberg.

The Numbers Game

Hitler's Willing Executioners is a book about perpetrators. If we ask the most obvious and immediate question — how many of such persons were there? — we are told:

- "tens of thousands" [pgs. 4, 24]
- "hundreds of thousands" [pgs. 8, 166]
- "certainly over 100,000" [p. 167]
- "500,000 or more" [p. 167]
- "might run into the millions" [p. 167]
- "the number of people who were perpetrators is unknown" [p. 11][7]

We are also informed that the number of Germans who are antisemitic "cannot be ascertained."[8] Yet, the major premise of the book is that the Germans were uniquely and uniformly antisemitic and that it is this particular form of German antisemitism, interwoven into the fabric of German society and culture, which accounts for the murderous quality and capacity of the German people.

If numbers are a problem when making assessments about the German populace in general, they are equally so when describing elements of the Nazi machinery of death. Police battalions, for example, are a major focus of the study. Among other things, we are told these auxiliary police units were complicit in "certainly over one million deaths and the number could be three times as high."[9] Assigning responsibility to police battalions for half the total number of Jewish victims of the Nazi slaughter means giving special but unspecified recognition to such units for deaths carried out by the special execution squads composed largely of SS personnel (i.e., the *Einsatzgruppen*) and the personnel of the extermination camps which the evidence suggests relied heavily on Poles, Lithuanians, and others from the occupied territories.[10] (Here, one also notes that if the assertion, cited earlier, is made that the Jewish slaughter says something about Germans that cannot be said of any other nationality, then reporting the frenzied orgy of bludgeoning, slashing and shooting of 6800 Jews by Lithuanians in Kovno is hardly a way to buttress one's point).

The battalions themselves are also the foci of specific numerical assessments. Police Battalion 101, the subject of extended discussion by Goldhagen, is composed of ca. 550 men; "assessing their backgrounds". Goldhagen states, "allows us to gauge how representative [they] were of other Germans and whether or not the conclusions drawn about them might also apply to their countrymen."[11] Having been forewarned that this is a major intent of the study, we are especially interested in what the lives of 550 police reservists can tell us about the views, attitudes, motives, biases or convictions of 65,000,000 Germans.

It turns out, however, that once again the data are a problem, "The biographical data that exist on these men are scanty, so only a partial portrait of the battalion can be drawn."[12] That portrait, we learn in an endnote, was constructed by first preparing a roster of the 550 men who were listed as members of the battalion on 20 June 1942 and then submitting their names and birthdates to the Berlin Document Center, which then determined the names of those who were members of the Nazi Party. Additional information was then culled from Party and SS files.

From these sources, Goldhagen is able to establish the ages of 517 members of Battalion 101, the occupations of 291, and the marital status of 96. The only other specific information he is apparently able to glean is that 179 were members of the Nazi Party and 21 were members of the SS. On the strength of these data — age, occupation, marital status and Party/SS membership — Goldhagen feels confident not only in drawing a social profile of the Battalion but also in projecting that profile onto the entire German populace. We know nothing about the educational backgrounds of these men, nothing about their religious affiliations,[13] nothing about any social club memberships they might have held, nothing about their income, their political views or any of a dozen other pieces of biographical information that might permit a tentative determination of just how representative of the general German populace these men really were.

Goldhagen, in fact, denounces Holocaust scholars for their failure to engage in precisely the endeavors he seems to relish most: reaching grand conclusions where the evidence is weakest. In a single paragraph and accompanying endnote, he dismisses Hilberg, Krausnick, Wilhelm, Davidowicz and Browning for having "created or countenanced ... erroneous stereotypes"[14] about perpetrators and of making "little mention ... of any aspects of their lives aside from the killing and their other operational tasks."[15] Simultaneously, Goldhagen observes that one of the sources (the Regimental Orders which were issued weekly and covered health, recreational, social and other matters) from which he has drawn extended conclusions about the "fullness" of the lives which the Battalion members led, contains "scanty information ... paltry in volume and variety in comparison to the reality of the stream of the Germans' daily actions while on duty or at leisure."[16] They are apparently not so scanty that they deter Goldhagen from making major findings of fact and judgment.

B.

Ultimately and regrettably, *Hitler's Willing Executioners* manages to accomplish precisely what its author asserts is the burden all Germans must bear. By finding that the whole of German society during the Nazi era was incurably antisemitic and thereby capable of the same murderous behavior as that displayed by the personnel who accompanied the SS execution squads, who manned the work camps and who directed the death marches, this book turns out to be as racist toward Germans as it accuses Germans in the Third Reich of having been toward Jews. This is unfortunate for several reasons.

In the first instance, not only is the evidence cited in support of this grand accusation highly selective; the book simply ignores the data that does not support its argument. In an effort to depict the German churches as thoroughly antisemitic, for example, it cites an infamous anti-Jewish declaration by a group of German church leaders who are described as "the Protestant Church leadership of a good part of Germany"[17,] without noting that these were leaders of the *Deutsche Christen* — that segment of a deeply divided German Protestantism which was most supportive of the Nazi regime and its ideology. Subsequently, the book argues that absent evidence of moral outrage or public dissent, the Germans must be seen as guilty of participation in the slaughter of the Jews[18] but it rejects this same "absence-of-evidence" argument when it is used to advance the claim that the German people were indifferent to the fate of the Jews. Silence in this latter instance, we are told, does not mean indifference but approval.[19] This, unfortunately, is a moral posture, not an empirical observation.

The supreme misfortune of such a blanket accusation lies in the fact that, a half-century after the occurrence, it falls largely on deaf ears. Increasingly, we find ourselves in an era and among a populace, both in and outside of Germany, which considers the preoccupation with the German Third Reich to be macabre, if not bizarre. However much we

Hyping the Holocaust

may wish to speak of guilt and responsibility, growing numbers of a post-World War II generation refuse to accept either. Insisting that all of their forbearers were murderers at heart is not likely to engender a sympathetic response from a large segment of today's German (or anyone else's) populace.

Guilt, either for the behavior of their nation a half-century ago but especially for any personal blame for what occurred, is a rapidly decreasing reality in modern German life. Responsibility, however, is a matter every sentient human being , German and non-German alike — must assume: responsibility for knowing what happened and responsibility for trying to ensure that it does not reoccur. Undifferentially tarring an entire nation with the same racist brush contributes to the very caricature of a people this book ostensibly wishes to avoid. To describe a totalitarian state and then blame its citizens for not behaving as though they were in a democratic society will strike many as neither fair nor informed.

· *Chapter 3* ·

Conditions for Carrying Out the Holocaust: Comments on Daniel Goldhagen's Book

by Hans Mommsen

· 3 ·

Conditions for Carrying Out the Holocaust: Comments on Daniel Goldhagen's Book

by Hans Mommsen

The attention that Daniel Goldhagen's award-winning book about "Hitler's Willing Executioners" is receiving, especially in the United States but also in other Western countries, teaches us that the emotional consequence of the German murder of the Jews still continues decades later. The book itself, intentionally provocative, does not really justify the newly aroused debate. It obviously lags behind contemporary research, and in large sections it rests upon insufficient evidence. It offers no new insight as to how to answer the question of how the collapse into barbarism, with the systematic liquidation of millions of guiltless people, became possible in an advanced and highly civilized country.

The emotional burden of every attempt to explain the SHOAH broke out in all intensity in 1960 as a result of the Eichmann Trial in Jerusalem, when in her report of the trial Hannah Arendt articulated the formula of "the banality of evil," which also rejected the conclusion — and also most of the research of that period — that the murder of the Jews was the direct result of a long-standing strategy of destruction. She evoked serious opposition when she stated that the antisemitic motive was only one factor in bringing the genocide to pass.

In fact the view then prevailed that Hitler planned the destruction of European Jewry from the very start, and had revealed his program step by step and finally accomplished it in wartime conditions. There was just as little question but that a significant part of the German population, especially those dependent upon elite functionaries, had to have known in one way or another about the systematic destruction of the Jews.

In the same way, research had concluded that the systematic destruction of European Jewry clearly was initiated on 31 July 1941, when

Göring gave Heydrich the assignment to initiate the "final solution to the European Jewish problem." The assumption was that only Hitler could have given such an order. Today this is doubted by most researchers, since it rests on an instruction that Heydrich had prepared for Hermann Göring, which he alone had signed — not to mention that fact that the instruction only applied to measures to be taken in the Jewish question after the war.

In the meantime there is a general consensus that there never was an official order to begin "the final solution." Similarly, before 1940 there was no longrange goal that went beyond a compulsory exodus of the Jewish part of the population, something that became less and less attainable as a result of the progress of the *Reich* to the east.

A qualitative sudden change was evidenced in defeated Poland, in first steps taken by Special Forces (*Einsatzgruppen*) A to D in territory occupied by the Soviets, for the first time in the late summer of 1941. Actions were taken to extirpate the Jewish populace, including women and children. Research ties this together with Himmler's visit in Russia, along with the euphoric confidence in victory he then communicated, which allowed him to expand by more than twentyfold the personnel available to implement extermination measures, in addition to involving the police battalions that had been stationed behind the lines for security purposes.

The radical break indicated here is not tied up with the instruction of the Gestapo chief, Heinrich Müller, to limit the exodus of Jews from occupied France to Morocco. This measure was connected rather to the changing plans for reservations, which the demographic planner Himmler and the national security headquarters were considering — among them the Madagascar Plan, the plan for a reservation near Lublin, and finally one yet to be established in the Polar Sea District.

There was not yet a generally applicable aim, such as the "at last discovered" solution of mass liquidations in Auschwitz and other death camps erected at the same time, although there was still a certain ambivalence in reference to the principle of "extermination by work" which Odilo Globocnik was applying in East Galicia and the General Government. The point of radical change to an all-European "Final Solution" was set by "Aktion Reinhard," the step by step liquidation of the Jews in the General Government area. This came after the various plans for reservations were shattered by the unexpected course of the war.

The latest research exposes an interaction between local and central functionaries, which finally led to a consensus of all participants that the

Jews found in German control should be liquidated. The issue was settled not just by ideological drives, but also by self-produced material and psychological compulsions. Thus the promise of the Soviet Union to transfer hundreds of thousands of ethnic Germans *(Volksdeutschen)* out of the Baltics, out of Wolhynia and Bessarabia into the Warthegau and other districts in the middle ground, gave the decisive impulse for the deportation of the Jewish populace and the erection of ghettos in the General Government.

Studying the complexity of these preliminaries gives cause for the historian of the Holocaust to show greater reserve in issuing sweeping generalizations. On the one side there is broadened research in the East European field in recent years , which shows that not only the SS and the more immediate terror instruments of the regime were involved in genocide through the politics of murder, but also the Army, the Foreign Office, significant portions of the internal and general administration, the police offices and the German railway system.

Today it is beyond dispute that the murder program could not have been accomplished without the active support of sections of the bureaucratic elite, even if the majority of them — whether through repression, through political naivete, or through moral indifference — took no account.

Certain knowledge or awareness in the carrying out of the criminal program was also discouraged among those who participated in the deportation of the Jews and their isolation from society and dispossession, or among those who directly profit thereby. Thus Raul Hilberg in his studies of the German railroad men who were responsible for the transports to Auschwitz, came to the conclusion that they performed their task of shipping Jews to the death camps for the most part without reflection. And Christopher Browning's epochal study of Hamburg Reserve Police Battalion 101 showed that the members of this unit, which had firsthand participation in the killing of Jews in occupied Soviet Union, even though they weren't primarily oriented to antisemitism had in no sense pursued their murderous work because they were compelled.

This moved Browning to the concept of "ordinary men," since the social composition of this group was not significantly different from the populace as a whole. Goldhagen takes another line, on the basis of the same materials but with less depth of insight, which imputes to the men of the Police Battalion a fanatical antisemitism through and through, which provides the motive and enthusiasm for sadistic violent acts against Jews — which did occur in isolated incidents. He counts in the inner circle of perpetrators one million Germans, derived from an erroneous reading of Ulrich Herbert's estimate of the number directly and indirectly involved in the deportations.

One can give Goldhagen credit that he has stubbornly worked out that the implementation of the Holocaust has been in an increasing measure the work of an alarmingly large number of persons, and that keeping the crime secret was not to be done. That at the same time it was not comprehended by the majority of the populace, or not in its totality, cannot be denied either. The social-psychological root causes for this are hard to put on a simple list. Attempts to quantify the number of actual collaborators and informed persons are accordingly of secondary significance, and only make more acute the problem of collective repression, alternating with the matter of insufficient information.

One can also doubt that a widespread knowledge of the crime would have evoked publicly relevant protests in the population. Thus far the attempt of Goldhagen to fasten the number of actual perpetrators upon the whole nation, and to impute to it a conscious assent to the Holocaust, is methodically of little use, particularly since it can only rely on estimates not empirically validated. In order to explain how the extermination process came to pass — and that is the issue, not primarily to attribute guilt — it is more meaningful to analyze the medium range of perpetrators, and thereby the mentality of the desktop perpetrator which was shaped by bureaucratic perfectionism. Contrary to Goldhagen, this has been done to a considerable extent, although not exhaustively.

The controversy over Goldhagen's book also touches on the question to what extent antisemitic attitudes, and also other historical ways of thinking must be calculated. It is beyond debate that the ground for a systematic Holocaust was prepared by a general antisemitic climate engineered by Goebbel's propaganda, and also by the threat to any who intervened for the Jews or sought to help them. Beyond that there were the strong antisemitic currents among members of the people of the east, especially the Ukrainians and Lithuanians.

Similarly, there can be no doubt that the latent antisemitism of the German upper class, opposed to assimilation, which was widespread in the military and bureaucracy of Imperial Germany, greatly increased the vulnerability in the Third Reich. Thus the generality followed without recognizable resistance Hitler's equivalence of Judaism and Bolshevism, and his call for a decisive race-war against the Soviet Union.

Nevertheless the actual shove toward the Holocaust came from fanatical antisemites, who numbered no more than 20% within the Party, but found in Hitler and Himmler and especially among the Nazi functionaries their prominent advocates. They had no sanctions to reckon with after the early resignation of Minister of Justice Gürtner, and with the readiness of the bureaucracies of the ministries to leave action on the "Jewish question" to the NSDAP. The minority of fanatical racist antisemites, constantly encouraged by Hitler and driven by the hope of commendation by the dictator, provided the true dynamic initiative that brought to the regime ever new impulse in what has been called "a cumulative radicalization." Consequently things came to a *kairos* in which, as Martin Broschat has described it, "the propaganda had to be taken at its word."

Meanwhile, it wasn't only the fanatical antisemitism of countless Nazi climbers, which broke through every restraint, that drove the constantly sharpening of measures directed against the Jews: rather, material interests played an important role. Many of the avowed executors like Adolf Eichmann or Theodor Dannecker first became reckless and fanatical antisemites in the course of their careers in the S.S., which let them forget an unfavorable vocational situation in civil life. They in no sense acted from ideological motives alone. You can search in vain for differentiating analyses of this kind in Goldhagen.

Where Goldhagen ever and again brings up the point that the persecutors had far less restraints upon them in dealing with Jews than in dealing with other racial enemies of the regime, this was — to the extent it applies — due to the fact that the Jews were the ones most regarded as outlaws. It is a fact that the Jews were evaluated as the lowest level of East European peoples. But that the Nazi killing machine, had it not been shattered early by the war's defeats, would have killed other peoples (including a-social or politically despised Germans) with the same lack of compassion as it did the Jews, is beyond denial. Independently, and this goes back to facts established by Götz Aly — a kind of compensatory effect was in play, as prominent executors who were at first chiefly involved in the colonization and demographic shift of ethnic Germans, turned to implementing the "Final Solution" of the Jewish question as their "positive" scheme, that is the realization of their gigantic colonization program for the East, even as the arrangements were shattered by the negative aspect of the facts of the war.

In the differentiating assessments of the newer Holocaust research, antisemitism appears as a necessary but by no means sufficient proviso for the implementing of the "Final Solution." The regime's structure, which put it in constant competition with dissolving institutions, to-

gether with a negative selection of political interests, impelled a cumulative radicalizing process in a direction at the end of which the liquidation
of the Jews was inevitable. In this process the bureaucratic-administra-
tive factor is at least as important as the compensatory hatred of the Jews
among the Nazi elite.

Against this background the question of the relationship of
antisemitism and Holocaust takes new form. It was not the radical
antisemitic demagogues like Julius Streicher or Joseph Goebbels, but rather
the antisemites of action who took the steps to systematic elimination
and provided an inner logic for the liquidation process of the Jews. It
required of course a social segregation of the groups to be persecuted, the
conditions of the war, and the general antisemitic indoctrination. This
compels also those who have survived to admit to themselves how thin
the patina of Western civilization is and how feckless the inherited moral
principles are in a net of illegality and political disorientation. This di-
rects attention to the moral presupposition of our culture and puts in
place the epochal demand which leads Dan Diner to speak precisely of
"a breakdown of civilization."

All along the line, the book by Daniel Goldhagen falls behind the
differentiated research discussion that has been sketched here. He is driven
by the determination to deny every mixture of ideological fanaticism, of
psychpathological aberration, of moral indifference and bureaucratic perfectionism, even of "the banality of evil," as an occasion for the Holocaust, for the greatest crime in human history. Instead he reduces the
cause of the Holocaust to the ostensibly high-strung German
antisemitism, which showed from the beginning the quality of
eliminationism and was thereby differentiated from the antisemitism of
other peoples and cultures.

Goldhagen thinks he can demonstrate a specific collective consciousness in the sense of Emil Dürkheim, and he speaks of "a German cultural
cognitive model of the Jews." He avoids, however, documenting this and
instead refers to a few works about the history of antisemitism in Germany, whose conclusions are not seldom lifted out of context and generalized one-sidedly.

Goldhagen simply issues the broadside reproach concerning previous research that it has repressed the joy of a whole people — that is, the
Germans, at the killing of the Jews. In this perspective, Adolf Hitler puts
in an appearance as a necessary result of German history, which has since
the end of the Middle Ages been shaped by a growing enmity toward the
Jews. In this the German people appear quite simply as the antisemitic

aborigines.

Goldhagen is obviously unaware that he runs the risk being accused of exchanging the usual antisemitic argument for a simple opposite, to perceive the German hatred of the Jews as historically inherited and an innate characteristic — even if he denies that in a Foreword which was sent along later.

Goldhagen sees "eliminationist antisemitism" tightly woven into German nationalism; therefore the individual German is not able to escape from this ideological entanglement.

Goldhagen also has no question about Hitler's direct intention to annihilate. He argues first from Hitler's well-known utterance in *Mein Kampf,* where in order to prevent defeat at war and the November revolution "12,000 of these corrupters of the nation" should have been held "under poison gas." Second, he argues from a police report which summarizes a speech by Hitler in the spring of 1920, in which he on the one hand advocates a "common sense antisemitism" and on the other stresses "stubborn determination to take the evil thing by the roots and tear it out root and branch" — an utterance that remained within the customary rhetorical antisemitism. Those are minimal proof that Hitler had concretely in mind the physical annihilation of the Jews. Martin Broszat's clever formula, that in the end the ideology "had to be taken sincerely," remains unnoticed, and also the question at what point the intention to annihilate systematically took over conclusively .

Goldhagen's schematic about antisemitism in Germany since early modernity and in the 18th and 19th centuries rests on an altogether too small and not always correct elaboration of the secondary sources (he refers at best only indirectly to primary sources). The derivation of "eliminationist" antisemitism, as he calls it, from the antisemitic proclamations of 1848 public meetings, and especially from the Hepp-Hepp riots of 1819, which were aimed against the enactment of Jewish emancipation, can hardly be convincing. It belongs to the account of the lingering Christian-religious condemnation of the Jews rather than to "modern" antisemitism.

Now no one denies the rise of extreme antisemitic points of view also in Germany, but rather the supposition that it indicated a bias that was widely spread and was also representative of Germany's political culture. That can fairly be denied. If Goldhagen's arguments were true, it would be utterly inexplicable why there was Jewish emancipation in Germany at all. With enthusiasm the author draws from a dissertation at Heidelberg, presented but unpublished, about the adoption of antisemitic stereotypes, the inflated thesis of an extreme antisemitism widely spread in Germany. It would be diversionary to pursue Goldhagen's statements in every instance, which exalt — in spite of the decline of the antisemitic parties — the antisemitic undercurrent that appeared in the Empire after 1878 as the dominant characteristic of German political culture after the turn of the century. At the same time he imputes an "eliminationist" manner to it, which again and again leads to grotesque errors of judgment.

The circumstance that antisemitic prejudices can sometimes be met in the Social Democrat constituency by no means justifies Goldhagen's sweeping claim that antisemitism had also taken over the working class. His analysis of the position of the Catholic sector of the populace and of the Curia on the "Jewish problem" is similarly distorted. Without doubt the churchly anti-Judaism played an important role deep into the 1930s, because in many respects it readied the path for Nazi persecution of the Jews. On the other hand, political Catholicism and substantial portions of the Catholic priesthood were decisive opponents of racist antisemitism and cannot in any case be added to the volume of the purported national storehouse of "eliminationist" antisemitism.

Just as little can the German nationalism of the 19th century be denounced as antisemitic, as Goldhagen bluntly claims. The thesis of Goldhagen that the national liberals, and not only its far right wing represented by Heinrich von Treitschke, were carriers of "eliminationist" antisemitism, is contradicted by the leading role of Jewish liberal politicians. Paradoxically, Goldhagen bypasses populist *(völkisch)* antisemitism, as it was propagated by Richard Wagner to Houston Stewart Chamberlain to Theodor Fritsch, although this was in direct line the immediate antecedent of Nazi racist ideology. More than that, he bends over to toss into one pot the anti-assimilationist antisemitism of conservative type, which entered into the Tivoli Program (1893) of the German Conservatives, with populist antisemitism. Nevertheless it cannot be denied that the former type contributed greatly to the fact that the German upper class — especially the military — raised no serious opposition to the Nazi persecution of the Jews, even if they didn't approve of the "methods."

At the same time Goldhagen argues — in clear disagreement with the interpretation of Shulamit Volkow, who portrays the antisemitism of the Wilhelm period as a dominant "cultural code" — that the antisemitism of the "German culturally cognitive model" was shaped by the intention of annihilation. This same argument is pursued further in respect to the time of the Weimar Republic. The early republic was certainly influenced by the massive populist antisemitism that exploded after 1917, which was supported by the Military High Command and found in Munich an extreme expression in the Soviet republic. This was no longer true of the period of stabilization, during which the antisemitic movement clearly ebbed, again to rise during the years of the economic crisis.

Populist antisemitism was represented in the front line by the *Deutschvölkischen Schutz- und Trutzbund* (German League Against Enemies Foreign and Domestic), which was a "front" of the All-German Union, as well as by the *Deutsch-völkische Freiheitspartei* (German Populist Freedom Party) which in 1922 split off as the right wing of the DNVP. The leader of the All-German Union, Counsellor Claß, in 1918 undertook to immunize the working class against the influence of the Social Democrats by mobilizing antisemitism, which — just like the Christian-Social Movement started by Court Preacher Stoecker in 1878 — collapsed all along the line, because antisemitism was not suitable as a means of mobilizing the masses.

At the time of its prohibition in 1921 the *Schutz- und Trutzbund,* which included practically the entire strength of organized antisemitism in the Weimar, tallied not more than 200,000 members. In comparison to the mass organizations — from the labor unions to the veterans — extreme racist antisemitism was therefore insigificant in numbers. It had however real significance for the *Freikorps* movement and above all for the neighboring Nazi Party, which recruited a high percentage of its nucleus from the *Deutsch-völkischen Schutz- und Trutzbund.*

Goldhagen's view, that antisemitism swept Hitler into power or that it was successfully used by him to mobilize the masses, therefore misses the mark. In the decisive campaigns from 1930 to 1932, which brought the break through of the NSDAP as a party of the masses, antisemitic agitation showed itself to be counter-productive, so that it was deliberately played down by the campaign leadership. Antisemitism played a minor role in the decision to vote for the NSDAP, as regrettable as it is that many sympathizers of the NSDAP were not disturbed by its exteme racist antisemitism and — especially in the conservative camp — saw in it only a childhood ailment which would in time disappear.

It would certainly be an error to depreciate the importance of antisemitism as a component part of the integral nationalism in Germany. The accusation that intellectual historians have done this is contrary to the facts. Antisemitism acquires its substantive importance above all as an intramural means of integrating the NSDAP, so that the heterogeneous ideological elements could be cemented together by one thing common to all: a picture of the Jew as enemy.

Goldhagen stands at the far wing of the intentionalists, and adheres to the thesis that Hitler always had a violent "Final Solution" in mind and implemented it as soon as the international conditions made it possible. He is not disturbed when, as his critics certify, the contrary results of research indicate convincingly that the regime had until 1940 no other "solution" in view except Jewish emigration. He depends chiefly on Richard Breitman's interpretation, without following it fully. The real question, why it came to a systematic genocide in connection with the activity of Special Forces (*Einsatzgruppen*) in the occupied Soviet zone, to the "Aktion Reinhard" is East Galicia and the General Government and to deportation of their Jews to the east at the urging of the *Gauleiter* (District Leader) of the *Altreich* District, thereby escapes his notice.

Instead, Goldhagen concentrates on the mindset of the perpetrators, and does this chiefly by dependence upon three case studies. The first deals with the history of Hamburg Police Battalion 101, with a glance at the role of the police battalions as a whole. The second case study analyses two Jewish work camps, the Lipowa Camp and the Airport Camp in Lublin District. The third study treats the complex of the "death marches." These studies are the cornerstone of the book, while the first two sections, although unusually loaded with propositions, exhaust themselves in comprehensive elaboration for which there are no archival or other unpublished sources and for which the secondary literature is only called up from time to time.

Because the participation of Police Battalion 101 in the "Final Solution" has been thoroughly presented by Christopher Browning (with detailed and very different analyses of the motives of the participants), this case study — although other police battalions are in part brought in — actually contributes no new results of research (although Goldhagen expressly claims that it does). Although he argues in the main from the same materials as Browning, Goldhagen reaches nearly contrary conclusions. Where he ascribes to antisemitic indoctrination a key role, Browning delivers — actually contrary to his original expectation — a thoroughly complex picture of individual motivations for murder, among which antisemitic indoctrination plays no dominant role. In that Goldhagen in an early review and now again portrays Browning, an expert and experienced Holocaust researcher, as naive and uncritical, it is all the more problematical that for long passages he follows Browning's treatment of the trial materials. On the other hand it must be noted that

Goldhagen's deeply prejudiced approach fully excludes any differentiational analysis that separates out the different constitutive factors that lead to action, all the more so because he stresses less an explanation of the action of individuals and much more the proof of their guilty behavior. He is no more interested in qualifying the generalization that the interrogations by the Hamburg judicial authorities are falsifications.

In respect to the Lipowa Camp and the Airport Camp — here too he depends chiefly on the documents from the Ludwigsburg Central Office of the Judicial Decisions of the *Länder* — Goldhagen endeavors to describe the brutal mistreatment of the Jews in as much detail as possible, while the relationship to "Aktion Reinhard" and its specific intentions is left untouched. Goldhagen's purpose is to display the unbelievable cruelty of the German perpetrators, which he specifically attributes to antisemitic attitudes. He is happy to be one of the first researchers to use photography as a source. In the papers of the Hamburg City Attorney contemporary photographs were also found. But he understands little of the difficulty in making precise the documentary relevance, the dating and the origin of photographs which as a rule survived in isolation. It is worth noting that the information about original source, so important for the historian, is neglected in the case of the photographs printed in the book.

The very high measure of violence, which Goldhagen substantiates especially in reference to *Aktion Reinhard,* is for him renewed proof of the deep antisemitic indoctrination of the Germans. He seeks to establish this further with the merciless cruelty of the guards who accompanied the Jews on the "Death Marches." But reservations must also be entered to the portrayal of the "Death Marches," as useful as it is and going as far as it does beyond the previous research. In the first place it wasn't only Jews who were victims of these senseless actions, and it is very relevant that the repeatedly terrorized civil populace ordinarily accepted the mistreatments and murders perpetrated before their eyes. Moreover, these occurrences are are to be related to the blood frenzy which the S.S. and Security organs, as well as the elite of the NSDAP, kindled in the last months of the war. Jews were the first, but not the only sacrifices. The excess of violence, which also was visited on Germans, derived from a mix of conditioning to brutality and the use of force and also a "go for broke" attitude of those who had burnt all their bridges behind them.

By accenting violence, sadism and murder lust Goldhagen is able to

derive the uniqueness of the Nazi persecution and annihilation of the
Jews. It is distinguished qualitatively from earlier antisemitic riots and
pogroms, which derived from a surplus of emotionalism but also ex-
hausted itself therein. The previous experience of pogroms evoked in the
Jewish councils of East Europe a false estimate of the mindset of the
persecutor, which attempted to accomodate it by passivity and submis-
sion. In the case of National Socialism it was however characteristic that
the "wild" attacks on the Jews were replaced by a well-planned and bu-
reaucratically perfected separation, pariah-making, and in the end annihilation. That corruption, joy in murder, and sadism also appeared, although Heinrich Himmler condemned it and Oswald Pohl as Chief of
Concentration Camp Policy attempted (unsuccessfully) to limit the use
of force, was not surprising under the given circumstances, and certainly
provides no explanation for the Holocaust.

Moreover, the portrayal of sadistic and brutal use of force releases in
Goldhagen a certain voyeurism, which serious research on the Holocaust
avoids through restrained portrayal of criminality, especially since it
changes easily into simple confusion and contributes little to real understanding. We may assume that Goldhagen is not sufficiently aware of
this effect, which apparently has contributed greatly to the mass sales of
his book. For him the evidence of sadistic terrorism is a decisive proof of
the extreme antisemitic stance of the perpetrator. Yet this is little convincing. Neither Himmler nor Heydrich nor Eichmann and many of
their underlings fit this category; and if we speak of the psyche of the
perpetrators, "Schindler's List" gives an impressive look into the multiple brokenness of the psychological-ideological concept of most of the
executioners.

Goldhagen emphasizes rather in billboard style that the Holocaust
represents the most extreme and most basic revolution "in the annals of
Western civilization," speaks of a "transformation of consciousness" of
the Germans, of the "implanting of a new ethos," and concludes with a
play upon words: in the end, "Himmler's culture" became "Germany's
culture." He sees in the implementation of the Holocaust the expression
of "a revolutionary transformation of German society," for which the
Nazi camp system was the god-parent.

Nevertheless it is doubtful whether it is useful to hypothesize the
regime's persecution of the Jews as revolutionary, quite apart from the
thereby necessary reduction of the social politics of the Third Reich to
the race question. The path is one of the working out of an exclusively
destructive — and not revolutionary — change, the termination of the

terminal politics of the regime in a human fiasco. It rang in Josef Goebbels' ears. By such a flourish the tragically trivial dimension of the affair as well as the repression of it even in a considerable part of the Nazi elite is totally removed from view, and only empty forms of words are left — such as this one, that it had to do with "a fundamentally new ordering of the social and human landscape of Europe."

The corrosive sharpness, with which Goldhagen ascribes to the Germans the pleasures of "demonic antisemitism," which places them altogether not only as accomplices but as enthusiastic perpetrators, is certainly not helpful in quieting resentments; it is anything but helpful in reaching a sober working through of the past precisely in the light of the present.

Scholars Answer Goldhagen

· Chapter 4 ·

"Ordinary Germans," The Holocaust, and Responsibility: *Hitler's Willing Executioners* in Moral Perspective

Roger W. Smith

· 4 ·

"Ordinary Germans," The Holocaust, and Responsibility: *Hitler's Willing Executioners* in Moral Perspective

Roger W. Smith

Assessment of guilt and responsibility in the Holocaust is complex, difficult, and disturbing, but, above all, necessary. Without it, there could be no moral understanding of the events and their lessons for the future, no sense of justice fulfilled or, more often, of its frustration, and no sense of closure. In 1947 the German philosopher Karl Jaspers attempted to enlighten us about the moral dimensions of the Holocaust. His book was called *The Question of German Guilt*. Fifty years later, the American political scientist Daniel Goldhagen returned to the subject in his passionate and ambitious work, *Hitler's Willing Executioners: Ordinary Germans and the Holocaust*.

A theory of responsibility that is adequate to its tasks must meet several minimum requirements. It must be clear, consistent, make appropriate moral distinctions, avoid collective judgment of entire groups, judge individuals but, at the same time, not rob them of personhood through dehumanization, and indicate what must be done for the sake of justice once the slaughter has ceased. Finally, a theory of responsibility should provide a framework of analysis that can illuminate not only the example of genocide that is under discussion, but other examples as well.

Jaspers largely met these requirements. Goldhagen's account, however, fails to meet any of them. The essay that follows explains how and why this occurs.

Clarity

If one is to take seriously a model of responsibility, its key terms must be clear, free from ambiguity to the extent possible, and their content steady rather than ever changing. In Goldhagen's account, the key terms are "the Germans," "ordinary Germans," and "eliminationist antisemitism." These are the foundations of his moral account, yet not one of them is clear, free from ambiguity, or used consistently.

A fundamental problem with his approach is the equation of "Germans" with "the Germans." "Germans" are individuals or groups of persons of German descent; "the Germans" refers to a whole people. Goldhagen is correct in saying that Germans, some of them Nazis, some of them not, carried out mass killing of Jews during the Holocaust. He estimates, for he has no solid evidence about how many participated in killing, that more than 100,000 Germans, and possibly as many as 500,000 or more, bear direct responsibility for the destruction of the European Jews. What he fails to mention is that the population of Germany in the 1930s was 65,000,000. Thus, while Germans helped to carry out the murders, most Germans did not; some Germans did, "the Germans" did not. Goldhagen, however places primary responsibility for the Holocaust, not on the Nazi regime, but on German national character, shaped, he says, by a century or more of virulent antisemitism. Given this kind of focus, "Germans" easily takes on a collective dimension, implicating all persons of German nationality. But Goldhagen does not leave it at that, repeatedly opting for "the Germans," a term that indicts a whole people for the crimes of specific persons and organizations.

Furthermore, Goldhagen treats "Nazis" and "Germans" as interchangeable, even though he knows that most Germans were not Party members; similarly, he equates "Hitler" and "the Germans" (pp. 139, 423). He also makes no distinctions between what one group of "Germans" has done and what other "Germans" *might do*. He asserts, for example, that the actions of a particular police battalion "can, indeed must be, generalized to *the German People in general*" (p. 402).

This brings us to "ordinary Germans," a term Goldhagen uses to suggest two points. First, that contrary to received opinion, those who carried out the mass slaughter of the Jews were not principally Nazi functionaries, but rather Germans who were typical of German culture and society. Second, "ordinary Germans" is a reply to Christopher Browning's *Ordinary Men*, in which he argued that the Germans in the police battalion that he studied killed Jews in Poland not because they were ideologically motivated, or because of hatred of Jews, but due to various situational factors. Goldhagen's counter-claim is that Germans killed, not because they were "men" responding to orders, peer pressure, and their own desire to advance their careers, but because they were "Germans."

His thesis is that German culture was such, that from the early nineteenth century on, to be a German was to hate, and want to eliminate, Jews from German society. Hatred of Jews was thus ordinary, expected, commonplace.

Goldhagen suggests that there were two kinds of "ordinary Germans," those who were in the Party and those who were not (p. 208). What they had in common was a worldview which demanded the elimination of Jews from Germany. Yet, unlike members of the SS, they were not "true believers," a distinction he does not spell out. In fact, for Goldhagen, "ordinary Germans" are simply Germans. However else they may differ in religion, politics, class, or education, they all share one characteristic — a worldview that Goldhagen labels "eliminationist antisemitism." But even if this were true, this kind of antisemitism includes, by Goldhagen's own account, two very different views of how to eliminate the Jewish presence from Germany. Whatever makes Germans "ordinary," it is not a common ideology.

"Eliminationist antisemitism" is thus fundamental to the argument of *Hitler's Willing Executioners.* Yet Goldhagen's definition of it is ever changing, his discussion is highly ambiguous, and his presentation comes seriously close to treating prejudice and murder as morally equivalent.

Goldhagen recognizes that there are at least two forms of "eliminationist antisemitism," but his definition of the concept shifts back and forth between them. This creates confusion in practice over whether a person who holds "eliminationist" views, wants to limit the rights of members of a group, or kill its members in whole or in part. Is one talking about discrimination or genocide?

The first form of "eliminationist antisemitism" would "eliminate all Jewish influence from Germany," but by means short of killing (p. 123). Yet where this type of antisemitism is involved, Goldhagen diverts attention from it by exploiting the ambiguity inherent in phrases such as "eliminationist ideal."

> To be sure, not all churchmen, generals, jurists, and others wanted to exterminate the Jews. Some wanted to deport them, a few wanted to sterilize them, and some would have been content to deprive the Jews "only" of fundamental rights. Nevertheless, underlying all of these views was an eliminationist ideal.

Any eliminationist view is morally repugnant, but it is not the moral equivalent of mass murder, a point that is obscured through the ambiguity created by Goldhagen's abstract terms.

One danger that the first version of eliminationist ideology presents, however, as a number of scholars have pointed out, is that it can produce an indifference to the fate of a people being subjected to death. Goldhagen, however, will have nothing of this argument: the Germans were not indifferent to the killing of the Jews; they welcomed it and many directly participated in the killings, "uncoerced, willingly, zealously, and with extraordinary brutality...." (p. 280)

The second form of "eliminationist antisemitism" is one that concludes, and acts on it where possible, "that the Jews *ought to die*" (p. 14). In principle, this could mean killing Jews in Germany only, or wherever Jews might reside. It is this murderous version of antisemitism that Goldhagen sees as being nearly universal in Germany, yet he acknowledges that it "cannot be ascertained ... how many Germans subscribed to it in 1900, 1920, 1933, or 1941" (p. 75).

Moral Differentiation

A theory of responsibility — at least, one that is clear, informative, and provides an adequate basis for moral judgment — will necessarily make distinctions on a variety of levels. It should tell us who the perpetrators are, the victims, the bystanders. It should distinguish between different types, and degrees, of guilt and responsibility — criminal, moral, political, and metaphysical. It should avoid collective judgment, in which whole groups, as opposed to individuals, are deemed guilty. And it should, at a very minimum, distinguish between actual and potential guilt.

Goldhagen's account falls short of each of these requirements.

The perpetrators were German, but not only German. The victims were Jews, but not only Jews. But for Goldhagen to take these facts into account would tend to undermine his explanation for the mass killings, namely, that it was the result of longstanding "eliminationist antisemitism" that predated the rise of Hitler, and resided "in the heart of German political culture, in German society itself." He adds that "among the German people ... support for the eliminationist project was extremely widespread, a virtual axiom" (p. 438). This claim leads him into collective judgment of "the Germans," with little attention to the type or degree of guilt of actual persons: the ultimate crime of the Germans is that they hated the Jews.

Further, Goldhagen makes no distinction between Germans who killed Jews and those who did not; his assumption, stated several times, is that, given sufficient opportunity, they would have. His judgment of Germans is thus collective in nature and revives the ancient, but long discredited, notion of collective guilt. It is worth pointing out that German antisemites held a similar view of guilt.

If for Goldhagen Germans cannot be bystanders to the slaughter of the Jews (but could be when other groups were killed, such as Gypsies), he leaves out entirely those bystanders — particularly the European and American governments — that are not free from responsibility for deaths in the Holocaust. But again, to condemn governments for not allowing Jewish immigration in the 1930s, for not making rescue efforts in the 1940s, and for not bombing the rail lines from Hungary to Auschwitz in 1944 (which could have saved 10,000 lives a day) would, apparently, dilute German guilt. To the contrary, by making proper distinctions in terms of types and degrees of responsibility, one places the Holocaust in a deeper, and more broadly human, perspective.

Throughout his work, Goldhagen erases distinctions and equates the dissimilar. Nowhere is this more pronounced than in his constant, mantra-like invocation of "the Germans," when it is clear from the context that he is talking not about "the Germans," but a particular individual or group of Germans. These turn out to be "Hitler," the "SS," the "Nazi leadership," or identifiable "perpetrators," all of whom have names. Here two illustrations will have to suffice:

> Once the mass slaughter began in the Soviet Union, attention could be diverted to the rest of Europe, and the extension of the killing elsewhere was but a matter of operational detail, logistics, and timing. The Germans had to concern themselves only with practical matters of organizing the genocide and with doing so in a manner that would be harmonious with their other strategic, economic, and transformative objectives ... (p. 156).

Surely, the relevant group here is not "the Germans," but rather the Nazi leadership and those charged with organizing the genocide. Elsewhere, he tells us that the SS was "the institution which more than any other organized and implemented the eliminationist and exterminationist measures" (p. 141), but then almost immediately starts to speak again of "the Germans."

The few distinctions that Goldhagen does make are largely implicit. They also rest upon omission: one side of the contrast is most often ignored. Further, the moral assessments he makes in these instances are significantly flawed, even bizarre.

Goldhagen's sharpest criticism, for example, is reserved for Christian clergymen and theologians; the Nazi leadership, with whom they are implicitly contrasted, initiated the mass murder of Jews, yet, astonishingly, come in for *no moral criticism at all*. Similarly, he implicitly contrasts the Nazi leadership and "ordinary Germans," but only the latter are morally condemned. Although he is right to condemn camp guards who engaged in "gratuitous cruelty," he fails to condemn the "desk murderers" such as Eichmann, who would never kill a fly, but were responsible for the deaths of millions. But, in the end, he abandons his implied distinction between the sadists and "ordinary Germans," for "where the opportunity to be brutal existed, German cruelty was nearly universal" (p. 377). Once again, we are back with "the Germans."

Consistency

A minimum condition for the validity of a moral theory is that the claims that lie close to the heart of the analysis be consistent. Goldhagen's theory fails to meet this test and does so in such a way that the thrust of the entire book is called into question. The basic problem is that Goldhagen offers two different, but conflicting, accounts of why Germans took part in the Holocaust.

One account stresses that Germans chose to kill Jews, that they did it willingly, that they killed or tortured apart from orders, that they acted as autonomous moral agents. In the police battalions, for example, men generally declined when offered the opportunity not to participate in killing operations. Goldhagen is here arguing against those scholars who stressed "obedience to orders," and those who put emphasis on social structure, or situational factors, as shaping outcomes. He summarizes this side of his argument by saying: Germans were "not robotic killing machines" (p. 266). Germans, in short, were autonomous, exercise free will, and committed the horrible acts they did because they chose to do so (p. 116).

Goldhagen, however, has an entirely different account that rests not upon choice, but rather social (more specifically, cultural) determinism. He signals this perspective on the first page of his book, quoting Tocqueville for support:

> No man can struggle with advantage against the spirit of his age and country, and however powerful a man may be, it is hard for

him to make his contemporaries share feelings and ideas which run counter to the general run of their hopes and desires.

Goldhagen argues that, due to the eliminationist antisemitism that was endemic in German culture and society, virtually every German shared common perceptions, cognitions, beliefs, and values that were genocidal.

> Genocide was immanent in the conversation of German society. It was immanent in its language and emotion. It was immanent in the structure of cognition (p. 449).

It was immanent, he says, because it is:

> incontestable that the fundamentals of Nazi antisemitism, the antisemitic brew that spawned Nazi thinking about Jews, had deep roots in Germany, was part of the cognitive model of German society, and was integral to German political culture. It is incontestable that racial antisemitism was the salient form of antisemitism in Germany and that it was broadly part of the public conversation of German society. It is incontestable that it has enormously wide and solid institutional and political support in Germany at various times ... It is incontestable that this racial antisemitism which held the Jews to pose a mortal threat to Germany was pregnant with murder (pp. 74-75).

Although Goldhagen does not use the term "cultural determinism," he explains how the process works. "An individual learns the cognitive models of his culture, like grammar, surely and effortlessly" (p. 46). Further, without "institutional support of some kind, it is extraordinarily difficult for individuals to adopt notions contrary to those that prevail in society, or to maintain them in the face of widespread, let alone near unanimous, social, symbolic, and linguistic disapproval" (p. 46). On cultural determinism in Germany, he has this to say:

> When a conversation is monolithic or close to monolithic on certain points — and this includes the unstated, underlying cognitive models — then a society's members automatically incorporate its features into the organization of their minds, into the fundamental axioms that they use (consciously or unconsciously) in perceiving, understanding, analyzing, and responding to all

social phenomena ... During the Nazi period, and even long
before, most Germans could no more emerge with cognitive
models foreign to their society ... than they could speak fluent
Romanian without ever having been exposed to it (pp. 33-34).

In this way, Goldhagen even comes up with an explanation of why
Germans during the death marches, when there was virtually no super-
vision, continued to kill Jews. Previously, he had used this as evidence of
choice, but now he states that it was the result of the "invisible coordination that common beliefs and values provide" in the "absence of central
coordination" (p. 400). His theory, to the very end, is contradictory. As
such, it is neither true nor false; rather it is incoherent.

Goldhagen's inadequate theory has major implications for the entire
argument of his book. If the behavior of Germans during the Holocaust
was determined by their culture in ways, as he suggests, that they could
not resist, then he *cannot hold them responsible* for what they did to the
Jews. Such a strong claim of determinism precludes responsibility. Indeed, it leads to the unacceptable claim that the Germans were simply
victims of their history. On the other hand, if he insists on German
responsibility, then he *must give up, or greatly qualify, his deterministic,
mono-causal explanation.* But this he is not prepared to do, nor can he
without his thesis collapsing entirely (p. 416).

It is possible to avoid the contradictions of his theory — some degree of social determinism and choice are compatible — but both his
claims about choice and about the group mind of Germans would have
to be greatly softened.

Personhood

A moral theory must pass judgment on those who engage in evil, yet,
however difficult it may be, avoid dehumanizing those it judges.
Goldhagen is aware of this: he rightly points out that too often explanations of the Holocaust deny the humanity of the perpetrators, particularly through viewing them as lacking the capacity to make moral choice
(p. 392). But, as we have seen, Goldhagen's own account invokes social
determinism to such an extent that it does turn Germans into beings
incapable of making moral choices. But that is only part of the way in
which Goldhagen reduces the Germans to beings unlike us (pp. 27-30,
460). The Germans are the *OTHER*: "Germany during the Nazi period
was a society which was in important respects fundamentally different

from ours today, operating according to a different ontology and cosmology, inhabited by people whose general understanding of important realms of social existence was not 'ordinary' by our standards" (p. 460)

It was inhabited by a people whose worldview led them to demonize the Jews, and when granted the opportunity, to kill them willingly, zealously, righteously. They not only killed them, they deliberately inflicted as much suffering as possible upon the Jews, engaging in unspeakable cruelties. They photographed Jews being humiliated, tortured, and shot, and sent the photographs home to share with their families. They celebrated over drinks the success of the just concluded "Jew hunts" in Poland. They brought their pregnant wives out to see the massacre of Jews. On the death marches, they went out of their way to inflict the maximum pain on the Jews, even though Himmler had ordered the violence to cease.

Of course, Goldhagen is describing the actions of some Germans only. But he does adhere to a version of collective guilt, and claims that even if most Germans did not participate in such acts, they would have if given the chance. It is not only what he says, but the constant repetition about German character and the cruelty that Germans are capable of, that leaves the reader with a thoroughly dehumanized view of 65,000,000 people.

Goldhagen does not judge the acts of particular persons, rather he dehumanizes, vilifies, even demonizes the German people. His account of the Germans turns, in fact, upon an inversion of the very attitudes that he condemns in nineteenth and twentieth century German culture. In his account, "culture" replaces "race," but the dehumanization is similar: the Germans/Nazis saw the Jews as a criminal race; Goldhagen sees the Germans as actual or potential murderers, lying in wait to kill Jews. To be sure, Goldhagen does say in a footnote that there is no "timeless German character," but that provides only cold comfort to potential victims living among them during the century or more in which they were inclined to commit genocide (p. 582, n. 38).

Genocide and Responsibility

Further, a theory of responsibility should provide a framework of analysis and assessment that can illuminate not only the example of genocide that is under discussion, but other examples as well. The facts will differ in each case — the killing may be carried out by special units, or by the population more generally; bystanders may be numerous or few; the technology of death may vary from machetes to starvation to gas ovens. But whether one is talking about the genocide of the Armenians, Jews, Gypsies, Bengalis, Cambodians, Bosnian Muslims, or Tutsi and Hutu, the same issues of responsibility arise, and must be addressed. When those issues are swept aside, or dealt with only in part, our understanding of genocide is greatly diminished; further, we have little basis for seeking justice for the victims, and little insight into the necessary moral and political reconstruction of the perpetrator state or society.

Even if Goldhagen's contentions about antisemitism and ordinary Germans were correct, these conditions (which can be generalized as a dehumanizing ideology that is widely accepted within a society) are neither necessary nor sufficient conditions for genocide. Nor is ideology the only issue that must be considered in assessing responsibility in cases of genocide. Moreover, the model of responsibility that undergirds *Hitler's Willing Executioners* fails even to illuminate issues of responsibility in the German case. It is, as we have seen, unclear in important respects, inconsistent, one-dimensional, appears to incorporate a version of collective guilt, and, as will be suggested in the conclusion, is incomplete, omitting questions of justice and rehabilitation.

Much of the inadequacy of Goldhagen's account stems from his unswerving focus on a mono-causal explanation of the destruction of the Jews. His moral theory is subordinate to, and derivative from, his belief that ordinary Germans willingly killed Jews, or would have if given the opportunity, because they had a thoroughly dehumanized view of them. His moral indictment is, first of all, of a worldview, for it is from this, he argues, that humiliation, cruelty, and death flow. But in identifying virtually all Germans with that worldview, he indicts an entire people. In so doing, he radically confuses criminal and moral guilt, and actual and potential guilt.

Justice

Finally, a theory of responsibility is incomplete if it does not tell us what is to be done in light of the violations that have taken place. What is required to restore the moral order? How is justice to be achieved? When genocide is involved, these questions, due to the number of victims and the need to prevent reenactment of similar killing, are all the more important. They also become more difficult: it may be possible to achieve justice where an individual has committed an individual murder, but how punish adequately those responsible for the deaths of millions? Such evil robs us of the capacity to respond adequately to it, whether through law or even finding the words to describe it. Nevertheless, both respect for the victims and the removal of genocidal potential from the society require that efforts be made to restore the moral order. The following actions, though none will be wholly successful, can contribute to a measure of moral healing and rehabilitation: punishment, restitution, reparations, the transformation of the political and ideological bases of a society, and moral atonement by individuals that begins with recognition of their guilt and responsibility and continues with a growing commitment to the preservation of life.

What is Goldhagen's perspective on the restoration of moral order after the killing has stopped? He has provided, after all, a searing indictment of "the Germans," the vast majority of whom, he claims, understood, assented to, and, "when possible," did "their part to further the extermination, root and branch, of the Jewish people. The inescapable truth is that, regarding Jews, German political culture had evolved to the point where an enormous number of ordinary, representative Germans became — and most of the rest of their fellow Germans were fit to be — Hitler's willing executioners" (p. 454).

But given this indictment, what does Goldhagen think should be done with such a people? Exterminate them? Punish them, in whole or in part? Attempt to create the conditions through which a society can rehabilitate itself, this time on the side of life?

Unfortunately, Goldhagen has nothing explicit to say about either the claims of justice or the steps necessary to transform "ordinary Germans" into persons "like us." His moral theory is radically incomplete. Worse, his whole account of the Germans places them outside the bounds of humanity, suggesting their proper status to be that of a pariah people, shunned by the world. Whether this was his intention is unclear; it is, however, the effect. Once one demonizes a group, the theoretical road back is almost impossible.

· *Chapter 5* ·

Daniel J. Goldhagen's View of the Holocaust

Yehuda Bauer

· 5 ·

Daniel J. Goldhagen's View of the Holocaust

Yehuda Bauer

No book on the Holocaust has caused the kind of public controversy that Goldhagen's *Hitler's Willing Executioners* has. Hundreds of thousands of copies have been sold in the US alone. Translations of the book have appeared and will appear in a number of languages. In Germany, a major public discussion took place in major papers, chiefly but not exclusively in the intellectual weekly *Die Zeit,* and in overflow lecture halls. It was clear from the outset, that is from the first symposium held at the Washington Holocaust Memorial Museum in April, 1996, that this would be the case.

Overwhelmingly, the public reaction in the United States was and remains positive; the less the commentator knows about the subject matter, and the more s/he is emotionally involved, the greater the enthusiasm. The professional historians, with some exceptions (Gordon A. Craig is the most notable one in the English-speaking world), and more especially the historians who deal with the Holocaust directly, have been overwhelmingly critical of the book.

There is no need to repeat Dr. Goldhagen's theses, as the book has by now presumably been read by most of those interested in the subject, and as the number of reviews has mounted to a near-deluge.

There is an assumption underlying his thesis: he believes the Holocaust to be explicable, and not, as Elie Wiesel and many others have stated, essentially a mystery to which we can never know an answer. On this issue, I completely agree with Goldhagen. If we cannot understand the Holocaust, we can never understand human history, because so much of it is murder and mayhem. Murder, whether individual or en masse, whether committed because of emotional reasons or as the outcome of rational calculation, or mixtures of both, is eminently human, common, and perfectly understandable — and condemnable. Sadism, killing of children and defenceless adults, tortures, humiliation, dehumanization — all these have been practiced by humanity since prehistoric times.

The Nazi addition to these practices — and it is true that the Nazis added refinements unknown in the past — is not qualitative. It is not the content of the murderous actions that is new, but the forms, which reflect our "advanced" stage of civilization. The Holocaust is not unique in this sense. Nor, one should add, are the numbers of its victims higher than those of some other mass destructions. Goldhagen's defence against mystification is cogent, although many historians, including some of the most important ones, will disagree with him on this issue. I do not.

The second point, which has to be stressed, is that Goldhagen places antisemitic ideology at the center of his explanation of the Holocaust. Again, in principle, I agree with him rather than with those, such as Hans Mommsen[1] and the functionalists, who emphasize the social stratification in a crisis situation, the political and economic background, and the bureaucratic machinery. In recent years, many authors dealing with the subject have followed this latter approach. Thus, for instance, Zygmunt Bauman[2] has tried to explain the Holocaust by holding "modernity" (a rather vague concept, I think) responsible, not antisemitism (though he counts antisemitism a *necessary* condition). Goetz Aly[3] thinks the explanation lies in the self-created constraints of the Nazis, as a result of their decision to reorganize the whole ethnic composition of Eastern Europe, in 1939-1941. The motivation for this reordering he believes to have been partly racist, or nationalist, partly economic and social, and power-political. The ethnic Germans were to "return" to settle the expanded Reich's eastern provinces in place of the Poles who were to be evicted. The Poles were to take the place of the Jews, who were squeezed into ghettoes, in order to be deported out of the German sphere of influence. When that did not work, the natural, solution was to kill them off. No Hitler order was needed for that, the bureaucracy knew very well what had to be done, says Aly. Other historians such as Christopher R. Browning[4] or Ian Kershaw[5], and many others, see a combination of factors at work, and do not take the extreme functionalist line.

All these authors, including those I do not agree with, have made important contributions to our knowledge, and their findings have to be taken into account — which Goldhagen refuses to do, because he has an overbearing attitude to the work of others, and because he offers a monocausal explanation: only eliminationist antisemitism was the motive. But however erroneous such an exclusivist position is, the renewed emphasis he puts on the ideological, antisemitic factor, is useful. Aly,

Bauman, Mommsen, even Raul Hilberg[6], cannot explain *why* the murder happened.

Hilberg has stated often that he preferred not to ask the big questions because he was afraid he would come up with small answers. His own masterful analysis of the German bureaucratic machinery that sent the Jews to their deaths does not explain why they did it. To paraphrase one of his most impressive examples: the bureaucratic steps the railway officials took to organize the trains that deported Jews to the extermination camps were exactly the same as the ones they used to organize German children's transportation to summer camps. But Hilberg cannot answer the question why they did the one rather than the other. Aly cannot explain why, if the Germans wanted to clear out Polish Jews in order to make space for German settlers on Polish territory, they sent Russian, French, Dutch, Albanian Jews to their deaths, or for that matter, Jews from Corfu and Rhodes. Bauman cannot explain why German modernity attacked Jews, and Italian modernity attacked Ethiopians — but quite differently; and of course Italians rescued Jews, by and large. Nor does he explain why the Holocaust occurred in modern Germany rather than in the modern totalitarian Soviet Union, or the very modern democratic United States. One does not have to take Goldhagen's explanation as the last word in order to see that antisemitic ideology played a crucial part, and the fact that Goldhagen redirected attention to antisemitism has to be valued positively. It is to his great credit, as my colleague and friend Israel Gutman said, that the discussion, in the wake of his book, will have again to deal with that central issue.

Why is Goldhagen's explanation simplistic? Let me first of all repeat what some other commentators have already said:

Goldhagen, in his book, ignores the social and economic traumas that afflicted German society in the wake of World War I. These were many: there was the destruction of the social fabric of pre-1914 Germany, with the attendant loss of personal, economic and psychological, security and identity — this applied mainly to the aristocracy, the bureaucracy, and the middle class generally. Or the fact that millions of mothers lost their sons and wives their husbands — and many others had to care for the wounded and the crippled.

France and Britain suffered proportionately similar losses, but they were the victors, and it seemed to some that the sacrifices had been worth it. Others of course protested bitterly at the pointlessness of the slaughter. But the conclusion that was generally drawn in these countries was "to study war no more." Pacifism spread. In Germany, however, the defeat added to the general feeling of despair, and one of the escape routes was into a burning, chauvinistic, desire for revenge. The inflation in the early Weimar years caused further social dislocations, with the loss of savings of the middle class and the peasants.

The Great Depression hit a Germany that had already had its fill of such disasters, and it hit particularly hard. All this does not exist in Goldhagen's description. After the discussion of the book in Germany, Goldhagen apparently revised his position somewhat and admitted he should have considered these aspects more than he did. But it is not the case that he has to improve his statements on these issues: quite simply, the book almost does not deal with them at all.

Critics have pointed out that Goldhagen does not explain how a supposedly general antisemitic norm in society translated itself into the actual murder. Here again I have to come to the defense of Goldhagen: surely, if there is a norm in society that requires the elimination of a group of persons, then, if the society's structure is so organized as to provide a rationale to the killing, it will be done. The addition of a dose of structural factors (which no intentionalist will deny) to a basic motivation does provide a sufficient answer. If the general motivation is there, accepted social structures sanction it, and a general order is understood to have been given, then a consensus will emerge, and it will be done. However, the question is whether there was such an exterminationist antisemitic norm in German society from the mid-nineteenth century on, as Goldhagen asserts.

Here he stumbles very badly, on a number of fronts. He does not seem to be acquainted — or at least he does not show it — with some pretty basic developments in German society in the nineteenth century. There was indeed what he calls eliminationist antisemitism, and its impact increased as the century matured. In fact, one could add a great deal more quotations to the ones Goldhagen presents. However, antisemitism came in different forms, and Goldhagen puts all of it in the same basket, including the liberal approach which wanted to see the Jews disappear by assimilation and conversion.

He quotes Uriel Tal's work[7], but Tal never said that liberal efforts to assimilate the Jews were the same as exterminatory programs. Despite his trenchant critique of German liberalism, Tal knew very well how to differentiate between someone who wanted to change his identity and someone who wanted to kill him. There were gradations between these two positions, and the vast majority of German antisemites did not even wish to abolish formal Jewish emancipation. Goldhagen makes much of the radical antisemitism of the Conservative Party in Germany; but in 1893, it only obtained less than 10% of the votes, whereas the National Liberals, among whom there were a number of ex-Jews, were much more important.

By 1912, the Social Democrats, with an explicitly anti-antisemitic program, were the largest party in the German Reichstag, and the Progressives ran very strongly as well. In Goldhagen's book there are no Social Democrats. Then again, the Jews had been fully emancipated with the establishment of the Empire, and though they were kept out of certain influential occupations, enjoyed an extraordinary prosperity. They were well accepted in middle class circles, and — this again has been pointed out in the discussion — they flocked to Germany from normatively antisemitic East European societies.

A book that appeared at the same time as Goldhagen's and was almost totally (and unjustly) ignored, John Weiss' *Ideology of Death* (Chicago, 1996), provides a different, and much more cogent answer to the problem of the impact of antisemitism in Germany and Austria. First, he differentiates clearly between the two countries, which Goldhagen does not, and shows that the Austrian version was much grimmer than the German. Second, and mainly, he argues that radical antisemitism — not always, but often, racist and murderous — became pervasive among the German and Austrian elites. These were the Court, the aristocracy, the industrialists, academia, the professionals, and the bureaucracy.

I do not see the Court and the aristocracy in Austria as antisemitic as in Germany, but the other elements appear to me be there. Whether or not Weiss exaggerates somewhat, it is indisputable that antisemitism, much of it quite radical, became fashionable among the German and Austrian elites. However, Weiss does not ignore Social Democracy (SPD) which, though originally based on theories which had strongly antisemitic overtones (Proudhon, Fourier, Marx, Bakunin), became the main bulwark against antisemitism in Germany. The 1912 elections were particularly crucial, because they seemed to threaten the imperial establishment with the possibility of an internal revolution by ballot. A coalition of SPD and Progressives might, at the next election, achieve a majority, and make Germany ungovernable by the right-wing pro-imperial parties. Weiss implies that Imperial Germany's contribution to the outbreak of war in 1914 may have been influenced by the fear of such a development. What this means from the perspective of Goldhagen's thesis is that a majority of German voters were prepared to vote for parties that were explicitly opposed to antisemitism. That could hardly have happened if there had been a general eliminationist antisemitic norm that pervaded all of Germany's society. There was a strong and growing element of such an influence among the elites, but even here it is difficult to talk of an unanimous approach. It is true that there were extremely widespread latent and overt, popular, antisemitic feelings — not "eliminationist" and not radical — among the masses of Germans. We have all learned from George Mosse[8] about these phenomena. But to speak of an eliminationist, or exterminationst antisemitic, all-pervasive, general German norm in the nineteenth and early twentieth century, is simply wrong. Goldhagen's thesis does not work.

But that is not all. Despite pervasive antisemitism (not necessarily eliminationist) among the elites, Jewish participation in World War I was, willy-nilly, accepted. Hitler's commanding officer, a lieutenant, who recommended him for the Iron Cross, was a Jew. Anti-Jewish propaganda, which led to a govermnent-inspired investigation as to how many Jews were serving in the German Army, was not successful. And the German Army was enthusiastically welcomed by Polish and Russian Jews, because it protected them from the antisemitic terror enacted by the Russian forces and because they behaved in a friendly and civilized manner. The Yiddish expression *"der Daitsh"* (the German) was one of respect and sympathy. Where was Goldhagen's norm, just over one decade before Hitler came to power?

The Weimar republic opened the gates to Jews to participate in politics and academia — though not the Army. It has already been pointed out that the Weimar constitution was written by a Jew, and that individual Jews achieved great prominence, especially in intellectual and cultural fields. Until 1930 there was a clear majority in the Reichstag of anti-antisemitic parties (SPD, the Communists, the Democrats), and non-eliminationist parties such as the Catholic Center Party which favored a Catholic, "moderate" antisemitism, that aimed not at the abolition of emancipation, but at the reduction of so-called "Jewish influence." Antisemitism of this kind was much stronger in Poland, for instance. The Nazis, one should remember, had been reduced to a small splinter group by 1928, and the German Nationalist Party, the party of the traditional antisemitic elites, was a definite minority. Where was Goldhagen's norm?

The last free elections in pre-Hitler Germany were held in November 1932, at the height of the economic crisis. In these elections, the Nazis lost 2 million votes, and 34 seats in the Reichstag. In a Reichstag of 584 members, the SPD, the Communists, the Democrats and the

Catholics together held 50.2%, or 293 seats; the Nazis and their German Nationalist allies had 41.9% or 248 seats, with the rest held by Right of Center splinter groups. In other words, a slight majority supported parties that were either explicitly non-antisemitic, or were "moderately" antisemitic, but certainly not "eliminationist" or exterminationist.

This does not contradict the statement that a very large segment of the population, including some in the SPD, both leadership and supporters, were "moderately" antisemitic in their general attitude, despite their official stand; but there was no political antisemitism there, and most certainly no eliminationist anti-Jewishness. And yet, Goldhagen is absolutely right when he insists, as against his critics, that by 1940-41 the general German society had become a reservoir for willing executioners or, if we prefer Hilberg's analysis, of bureaucrats who would be perfectly comfortable to use their very considerable skills and creative initiative, to put into practice, as a matter of bureaucratic routine, genocidal policies — or both. The argument between Goldhagen and Browning on this point is one of estimates — Browning believes the percentage of those who opposed the genocidal campaign was in the neighborhood of 20%; Goldhagen says it was nearer 10%. In either case, the statement that the vast majority of the German population was willing to be recruited for the murder of Jews stands. This has been said time and time again by a number of historians, Israel Gutman and myself included, and the fact that Goldhagen disregards the fact that he is not the first to say it is neither here nor there. The point is that he is right.

The real question then is this: if, in 1932, the Nazis and their radically, but not murderously antisemitic allies were supported by some 42% of the electorate, whereas non-Nazi parties received 58%, including over 50% of outspoken opponents of Nazi who were either clearly anti-antisemitic, or only moderately antisemitic (i.e. opposing even the relatively moderate step of disenfranchising the Jews), how did it happen that by 1940-41 the overwhelming majority of Germans became a reservoir for willing murderers of Jews? That is the problem, and not a useless discussion about norms, that did not exist. Goldhagen does not ask the question; therefore he cannot give an answer.

I believe, though, that there *is* an answer. In order to provide it one has to, first of all, rid oneself of the ideology of anti-Germanism, and give up the notions of pervasive eliminationist antisemitic norms in Germany. On the other hand, one has to recognize that any valid model must explain why it happened in German society and not, despite murderous antisemitism, in Russia or elsewhere. In other words, one has to deal with German specificity.

It appears that when an intellectual or pseudo-intellectual elite with a genocidal program — explicit or implicit — achieves power in a crisis-ridden society for economic, social and political reasons that have nothing to do with the genocidal program, then, if that elite can draw the intellectual strata to its side, genocide will become possible. By intellectual strata I mean, basically, what John Weiss describes as elites — upper-class social groups, army, churches, bureaucracy, the doctors and the lawyers, industrial and commercial elites, and especially the university establishments that provide all the rest with the necessary ideological tools. The intellectual elites will not necessarily support the genocidal program, but will identify with the regime that promises a utopia, including major economic, social and national benefits. In so doing, they will be more than willing to execute any policy that will be presented to them as conducive or essential to the achievements of these benefits. A general social consensus will thus be created with the help of these elites, and with the help of this sanction lower-class and general participation in the genocidal program will become attainable. This is what appears to have happened in Germany, after the elimination, by murder and terror, of tens of thousands of opponents of Nazism in the thirties. The concept of a consensus is absolutely central to this line of explanation. It also makes the behavior of, for instance, police battallions, such as battallion number 101, around which Browning[9] and Goldhagen wrote their books, much more intelligible.

The very prevalent types of latent or overt, non-murderous, antisemitic attitudes in the general population, the result of Christian antisemitism that had dehumanized the Jews for many centuries — though never translated into a genocidal program by Christian society — prevented any serious opposition to the Nazis once they had decided to embark on the murder of the Jews. Whether this model works not only for the destruction of the Jews at German hands is something that may be worth examining further.

It may also be worth examining some parallels: no one will argue that in 1926 or 1927 the overwhelming majority of Soviet citizens were ardent supporters of the Bolshevik rule. But there can be no doubt that in 1941 and 1942 millions of Soviet soldiers went into battle with the cry *"za Stalina"* (for Stalin) and that the communist regime was wholeheartedly supported by most people there. Similar examples can be quoted from other places and other times. The exact mechanics of change leading up to these phenomena have not been properly researched, and

Goldhagen cannot be faulted for not relating to them. But he could not do that anyway, because he is not aware of the problem. He missed the really important questions.

In effect, by arguing for a general social norm of murderousness towards the Jews, Goldhagen lets off the hook the particular and very specific forces that did, in fact, advance radical antisemitic views. This is true of the academics, this is true of the churches, this is finally true even for the Nazis themselves. After all, if all these, and others, were the victims of a culturally inherited social norm, they cannot be blamed for drawing the logical conclusions, can they?

So much for eliminationist antisemitism as a general norm of German society.

Many critics have already said: the book is without a general European context. If one wants to explain why the Holocaust happened in Germany and not in France or Russia, one must compare the situations between these countries. If I understood him correctly, Goldhagen argues that he did not have to do that precisely because it happened in Germany, and therefore only Germany was relevant to his project. This is peculiar, coming from a social scientist, and it is the basis of accusations against his Harvard tutors for not having drawn his attention to these grave methodological errors; they should have known better. After all, I am not exactly being original when I point out that Germany is located in Europe and its whole history is one of interaction with its neighbors — in the intellectual and ideational-sphere as well as in others. In addition, as I have tried to show, his thesis does not work as far as nineteenth-century Germany is concerned, so a comparative approach becomes even more necessary.

There is no evidence in the book that would show that Goldhagen knows languages other than English and German, or that he is acquainted with more than basic European history. What he calls eliminationist antisemitism was much more in evidence in Russia than in Germany, in the last century. The views of the elites, and the general attitude of the population, all pointed in the direction of an eliminationist antisemitism. Why did it therefore not happen in Russia? Well, one might argue that it almost did, but that the rise of communism in Russia may have prevented it. In any case, if one argues as Goldhagen does one must relate to the problem, and he does not. The same applies to at least two other European countries — France, and Romania. In France, in the last part of the nineteenth century, a truly eliminationist antisemitism became one of the main distinguishing marks of a violent nationalistic mindset.

In Romania, the murderously antisemitic forces came into power in 1938, and again in 1940, and the result was the mass murder of some 300,000 Romanian Jews, very largely by Romanian forces, albeit in alliance with Nazi Germany and with the participation of the infamous *Einsatzgruppen* (the *Einsatzgruppe* under Otto Ohlendorf). Lithuanian, Latvian and Romanian (and other) massive participation in the most brutal killings would, according to Goldhagen's thesis, indicate the existence of an eliminationist antisemitic norm in those nations. For Romania, this may actually be not far from the truth. But in that case there is nothing very unique about the Germans. Others had these eliminiationist impulses as well, but it happened in Germany, not elsewhere. And again, Goldhagen's theory fails there; one has to look for the special reasons why it happened in Germany in much more sophisticated and differentiated manner.

I don't want to linger too much on the three parts of his book where he produces factual material to substantiate his argument that there were large numbers of willing executioners. In fact, I think there were many more such people than even he imagines, including large numbers of ordinary *Wehrmacht* soldiers. His examples are in part, as others have already said, repetitions of what Browning has shown in his *Ordinary Men*. Goldhagen has more of the same, arguing against Browning in a way that one had better not comment on. But his view that one deals there not with ordinary men but ordinary Germans has, as I have tried to show, some merit. Except that his attempt fails to show what made Germans more adept at murdering Jews than Italians, French or Russians. His example regarding slave labor camps is rather weak, because there he involves people who were actually within the orbit of the SS. His description of one death march is the best part of the book, I thought. There may be little new in the general description, but the details and the way he describes the attitude of the murderers is powerful and convincing.

There is an overall problem, though, which is worth pondering upon: there is a danger that the Goldhagen thesis might boomerang. Sooner rather than later it will become obvious, beyond the circle of experts, that his explanation for the phenomenon of masses of willing executioners is mistaken, and that his anti-German bias, almost a racist one (however much he may deny it), leads nowhere. There then may come attempts to deny the very fact that such masses of murderers were easily recruitable from the German population. And when people realize that his attempt to explain all that by eliminationist antisemitism as a general social norm in Germany is equally erroneous, there may again come a denial that antisemitism is indeed the central element — though not the only one — in understanding the Holocaust. And then the question may be asked — it has already been put by some critics — what, after all is the difference between the murder of the Jews on the one hand, and all the others on the other hand? Is it not the same thing? Goldhagen cannot explain the Nazi murder of the Gypsies, the Poles, the Serbs, etc., by antisemitism.

A differentiated approach that recognizes the special position of antisemitism in Nazi ideology, but sees the connection that has with their overall racist and nationalistic program of reordering the map of Europe, is essential. That would explain why the Jews occupied such a central part in Nazi ideology, and why therefore the Nazi attitude to the Jews was indeed different from that towards others; but it would, at the same time, clarify the reasons why horrible mass slaughter was committed against other populations as well. It would then become obvious that the fate of the individuals, insofar as they were murdered, was the same, whether they were Jews, Poles or anything else, though the Jews definitely occupied the lowest rung, and were tortured and humiliated beyond anything the others had to suffer. Yet the Nazi attitude to the different groups was different. Yet again: Goldhagen never asks these questions. No wonder he cannot answer them.

Lastly, one has to ask why the book has been such an outstanding success. The tremendous efforts by the publisher cannot by themselves explain it. Nor can one be satisfied with the explanation that for many Jews, and many veterans of World War II, the book is a godsend: we always knew, many are saying, that the Germans were no good; here at last comes a gutsy young man who says it loud and clear. Jews and war veterans are, after all, minorities.

I believe the real reason is the very simplicity of the argument, its manichaean (black and white) character. A complicated phenomenon is seemingly explained in the most simple fashion: the Germans killed the Jews because they wanted to; they wanted to since the mid-nineteenth century, and maybe before that, too. And that's all there is to it. People don't like complicated explanations, they don't want diffentiated analyses, they want simplicity. Goldhagen gave it to them.

Goldhagen, and some of the members of the public who love him, are unhappy when they hear that one should show humility when approaching the Holocaust, a humility which he unfortunately failed to show. I cannot recollect that any of the historians who deal with the Holocaust approached their colleagues, never mind their subject, with an overbearing attitude. Goldhagen is a talented, promising academic. What a pity.

I do not think Goldhagen's book will make it into the Pantheon; but his faulty thesis provoked a discussion about essentials, and for that at least he should be thanked.

· *Chapter 6* ·

The German Resistance,
The Jews, and Daniel Goldhagen

Peter Hoffmann

· 6 ·

The German Resistance, The Jews, and Daniel Goldhagen

Peter Hoffmann

i.

In blanket statements the author of *Hitler's Willing Executioners* declares:

> The pre-genocidal eliminationist measures of the 1930s, the stripping of Jews' citizenship and rights, their immiseration, the violence that Germans perpetrated against them, the regime's incarceration of them in concentration camps, and the hounding of them to emigrate from Germany — the sum of these radical measures did not incense, or produce substantial opposition among, those who would eventually form the major resistance groups. Indeed, in the view of the foremost expert on the subject, Christof Dipper, the Gestapo's evaluation of the captured July 20 conspirators (based on the conspirators' own statements during interrogation), accurately depicts them as having fundamentally shared the regime's conception of the Jews, even if they differed on how the Jews ought to have been treated.[1]

And:

> By and large, those in the opposition and resistance to the Nazis were not moved to opposition by a principled disapproval of the elimination of the Jews from German society.

Amid reiterative verbiage, Goldhagen claims a

> glaring absence of significant protest or privately expressed dissent, especially principled dissent.

He cites Berthold Count Stauffenberg as testifying for himself and
for his brother Claus that they had considered the concept of race sound
and promising. He mentions Nikolaus Count Üxküll as "speaking for
most of the members of the non-communist and non-socialist resistance",
and as having

> summarized the intentions of the largest and most influential
> resistance group, the conservative and military opposition which
> was organized around Stauffenberg and Carl Goerdeler: 'We
> should hold on to the concept of race as far as possible.' In Nazi
> Germany, affirmation of 'race' as an organizing principle of so-
> cial and political life was to accept the foundation of the regnant
> cultural cognitive model of Jews, since the two were intertwined.

Dietrich Bonhoeffer is accused of having initiated "one of the central documents of the resistance to Hitler" with an appendix called "Pro-
posals for a Solution of the Jewish Problem in Germany".

The author of *Hitler's Willing Executioners* declares Dipper the "foremost expert on the subject" and testifies to his "accuracy", but he has not
examined Dipper's sources, nor any other published or unpublished
sources, nor the researches of dozens of specialists.[2]

When Goldhagen goes on to speak of the "glaring absence of significant protest or privately expressed dissent, especially principled dissent,
with respect to the treatment and eventual genocidal slaughter of the
Jews", he demonstrates his own ignorance of the subject on which he
pronounces his judgements. He cites his "foremost expert" to contend
that here was proof that the conspirators agreed "in principle with
antisemitism", but "rejected the methods of implementation". Then,
strangely, he concludes that the conspirators had no objection to "the
eliminationist persecution and, by and large, even the extermination of
the Jews".

What is agreement "in principle" (especially during interrogation by
the Gestapo), coupled with a "rejection of the methods of implementation"? Rejection of the practice makes approval of the theory irrelevant.
Goldhagen's allegations are refuted by the record. Goldhagen could have
examined the degrees to which resisters rejected anti-Jewish persecution,
rather than resort to sweeping, thoughtless falsehoods. He would have
found a range of reactions from anti-Judaism, coupled with rejection of
violence, to a gradual change in individuals' beliefs and persuasions. He
would have found the "principled dissent" which he declared to be lack-

ing. He would have found that the persecution of the Jews was a central issue and motive for the resistance, and that many resisters are on record as having given their lives above all because of the treatment of the Jews.

ii.

In the conditions of the National Socialist dictatorship — under permanent "emergency" decrees suspending civil rights and liberties; Hermann Göring's "shooting decree"; concentration camps; insidiousness law; special courts with extraordinary jurisdiction and no appeals; death penalty for damaging the reputation of the government and the NSDAP[3] — only muted reactions to the anti-Jewish measures could be expected.

The responses of the resisters who later contributed to the insurrection of 20 July 1944 represent a spectrum of reactions. Those whom Goldhagen denounced by name shall be discussed below. They were all hanged for their part in the conspiracy, except Claus Count Stauffenberg, who was shot on 20 July 1944.

The theologian Dietrich Bonhoeffer acknowledged in 1933 that the state had the right to determine the conditions of citizenship. But he was outraged at the perversion of justice of the Nuremberg Laws of 15 September 1935, which declared that only persons "of German or kindred blood" could be citizens.[4]

Ulrich von Hassell was appalled by the Nuremberg Laws, as his daughter noted in her diary on 18 September 1935. He condemned the laws as signifying "for our country the end of its culture"[5]. He recorded his outrage at the November 1938 pogrom in his diary under 25 November 1938:

> But my chief concern is not with the effects abroad, not with what kind of foreign political reaction we may expect — at least not for the moment. I am most deeply troubled about the effect on our national life, which is dominated ever more inexorably by a system capable of such things.

Hassell's published diary — thus far only the portions from September 1938 to July 1944 have been published — refers to the situation of the Jews 43 times.[6]

Berthold Count Stauffenberg said to his interrogators in the days before his execution that he and his brother Claus had initially approved of the greater part of National Socialist internal policies, among them "the racial principle". But he meant nothing more sinister that to deprecate racial mixing, for he concluded that "the fundamental ideas of National Socialism had in practice all been perverted into their opposites"[7].

The 20-July-1944 conspirators' draft "Policy Statement", of which Carl Goerdeler in court declared Colonel Claus Count Stauffenberg to be the author, stated among the "principles" and "aims" of the new government that the persecution of the Jews, "which has been carried on in the most inhuman and unmerciful, deeply shameful and never to be repaired forms" was to be halted at once, and that those responsible for the murder of the Jews would be punished[8]. In a similar statement the plotters said: "What is decisive for us is that we no longer tolerate impudent criminals and liars dishonouring our nation and soiling our good name. [...] We had to act under obligation of the conscience."[9]

iii.

Dietrich Bonhoeffer, in a lecture on "The Church and the Jewish Question" in Berlin in April 1933, publicly uttered his reservations against subjecting Jewish persons to special legislation. Bonhoeffer confronted the practice of the government's anti-Jewish measures in his lecture, in response to the first anti-Jewish measures of the new regime. He said that no doubt "one of the issues which our state must manage is the Jewish Question, and no doubt the state has the right to follow new paths here". Bonhoeffer acknowledged the sovereignty of nations in matters of citizenship. But in the same lecture Bonhoeffer described levels of Church action toward the state, particularly regarding the fate of the Jews. At the first level, the Church must monitor state action to ascertain its legitimacy and conformity with the will of God that the state must provide order, and it must ascertain that state action did not infringe upon the preaching of the Gospel; at the second level, the Church must serve and help any victims of state action and seek to alleviate hardships; but "if the Church sees the state failing in its function of creating law and order, that is, if it sees the state producing without restraint too much or too little order and law", then the Church must "not merely dress the wounds of those who come under the wheel but must get hold of the wheel itself"[10].

Bonhoeffer therefore, in April 1933, envisioned the overthrow of the Hitler government in connection with the "Jewish Question". In September 1933, at an ecumenical meeting in Sofia, Bonhoeffer tried unsuccessfully to move a resolution against the Hitler government's anti-Jewish policies as a whole. He only got a resolution adopted declaring the elimination of persons of Jewish descent from church offices a "denial of the explicit teaching and the spirit of the Gospel of Jesus Christ". The Bishop of Chichester, Dr. George K. A. Bell, remembered in 1945 that Bonhoeffer's own position was not limited to that issue. On the contrary, Bonhoeffer, at the age of only twenty-seven, had understood "as few others understood that the attack on the Jews was an attack on Christ, as well as an attack on man". Bonhoeffer was practically the only one who insisted that his Church take a position on the Hitler government's anti-Jewish policies as a whole. He found himself in opposition to all his friends whom he respected and became uncertain that he was right and all others wrong. He retreated from a brilliant university career, accepted a position as pastor of the German Lutheran community in London and served in that position from October 1933 to April 1935[11].

After his return from London in 1935, he expressed his condemnation of the government's persecution of the Jews openly. At the Old Prussian Confessing Church synod at Steglitz on 24 and 25 September 1935, immediately after the promulgation of the Nuremberg Laws, he demanded that those who professed to be Christians "open their mouths for the dumb", and that the synod take a fundamental position for the Jews.[12]

During the war, in a sinecure in the military counter-intelligence branch (OKW/Amt Ausland/Abwehr), Bonhoeffer continued to try to help Jews. In a memorandum of October 1941 he invoked the Nuremberg Laws to try to protect from deportation descendants of mixed Jewish-Christian marriages.[13] In 1942 and 1943, Bonhoeffer and others drafted "Notes for Pastors and Elders on the Treatment of the Fifth Commandment". The "Notes" denounced the "solution" of the Jewish question by "eliminating" and "liquidating". All pastors of the Old Prussian Confessing Church were instructed by its synod's Council of Brethren to read from the pulpits on Repentance Day in November 1943: "Woe to us and our nation if it is held to be justified to kill men because they are regarded as unworthy to live, or because they belong to another race." The drafting committee included Dietrich Bonhoeffer, who worked on the draft three weeks before his arrest (5 April 1943), and Peter Count Yorck, also one of the chief anti-Hitler conspirators. Bonhoeffer was arrested in April 1943 as a result of a rescue operation in which he had participated.[14]

Goldhagen says that a memorandum by Constantin von Dietze was "one of the central documents of the resistance to Hitler"[15] The "central" documents are, of course, first of all, the policy statements prepared by those (with whom Dietze was only indirectly associated) who attempted to overthrow Hitler.

Dietze was in a discussion group with Carl Goerdeler, the former Mayor of Leipzig, and Goerdeler's subsequent biographer, Gerhard Ritter. This "Freiburg Circle" of opponents of the regime was initiated in 1938 in an immediate response to the pogrom of that year.[16] In the late summer of 1942 Dietrich Bonhoeffer, acting on behalf of the illegal Confessing Church leadership, asked the group to prepare a paper for ecumenical discussions after the war; the paper was completed in January 1943. It contained appendices dealing with law, education, economics and the social order. Dietze wrote an appendix on the Jewish Question. There is no evidence linking Bonhoeffer to the contents of Dietze's appendix, beyond Bonhoeffer's general request of a discussion paper. Without citing any evidence, Goldhagen declares that this document was "prepared at the beginning of 1943 at Dietrich Bonhoeffer's initiative" with obvious though unspoken implications.[17] But while Bonhoeffer's theology was not free of traditional elements which included, in his early years, what has been called "conversion theology" and Christian "triumphalism", his and Dietze's position were worlds apart.

In his appendix Dietze said that the existence of races was a fact; that racial barriers in all Christian churches in the world were not contrary to the Christian faith; that nations had no right to set themselves above a nation which God was punishing, but that Christians were obliged to meet all humans in the spirit of love; that violence by one nation against another was a wrong before God; that measures which the state must take in order to protect a nation from the pernicious influence of a race must be guided by justice and ethical responsibility. Dietze condemned the Nuremberg Laws of 1935, the subsequent and frequently illegal and arbitrary police measures, the pogrom of 1938, and the deportations, mistreatment and "systematic killing of hundreds of thousands of persons solely on the basis of their Jewish descent". Dietze's memorandum demanded that all Jews who had left their homeland since 1933 must be allowed to return; that the state must abandon the Nuremberg Laws, and equally all special legislation, since there was no danger from the relatively small number of Jews still in Germany or likely to return; that an international convention must regulate the rights and obligations of Jews in all states which would treat them as foreigners but guarantee them freedom of religion, education and economic activity; that Jews who were not citizens of the country they lived in must be naturalized if they could offer good reasons, particularly a presence of their families for several generations, and accomplishments benefitting the nation in which they lived. No doubt these stipulations, directed against Jews, and reviewed after "Auschwitz", cannot but be considered insensitive, indeed threatening to Jews throughout the world.

iv.

A moderately detailed examination of the record of Carl Goerdeler, the Mayor of Leipzig (1930-1936) and Reich Prices Commissioner (1931-1932, 1934-1935), the civilian head of the conspiracy to overthrow Hitler in Germany, reveals the exact opposite of what his detractors say.

Goerdeler recalled in 1944, after he had been sentenced to death and while awaiting execution, that he had initially worked loyally with the National Socialist government and its functionaries. Since he had, in 1935, in an interview with Hitler, seemingly won the dictator's support for his own view on economic policy against a powerful rival, Economics Minister Hjalmar Schacht, Goerdeler was under the illusion that, given the opportunity, he would be able to persuade Hitler to end the war. But he had in fact intervened, in full formal dress, in the company of Deputy Mayor Ewald Löser, against actions by the National Socialists' Party militia, the SA (Stormtroopers), when these harassed and attacked Jews and businesses belonging to Jews on April 1, 1933 during the government-organized nation-wide "boycott", and he had personally protected Jewish furriers in Leipzig-Brühl against SA thugs and looters, "putting an end to the lawless goings-on". Also in the first weeks after Hitler's appointment as Chancellor, Goerdeler used the Leipzig police to liberate Jews who had been detained and beaten by the SA. In the following years, he stopped or impeded anti-Jewish measures in Leipzig wherever he could, although he could not prevent all anti-Jewish measures. Goerdeler could not change the law that prevented approbation of Jewish physicians, but he confirmed the legal protection of those whose approbations preceded the law, against the efforts of National Socialists to exclude all Jews from practice. He followed a similar procedure concerning dentists.[18]

The files of the Leipzig City Archives contain correspondence and minutes concerning restrictions for Jews in the use of public baths. In a reply to a complaint, the new National Socialist Deputy Mayor, Rudolf Haake wrote under the date of 19 August 1935 that he (he used the pronoun "I") had accepted the justification of the decree prohibiting Jews from the use of public baths in which they would come in contact with non-Jewish users. Goerdeler's involvement in the matter, although his ultimate responsibility as Mayor is clear, appears to have been limited to answering an inquiry from the Saxon section of the National Conference of Municipalities on 19 September 1936. He wrote (using the passive voice in the third person) that from the end of July 1935 Jews had been prohibited from using the Leipzig municipal summer baths and indoor pools and other communal baths.

Goerdeler has also been accused of anti-Semitism because he regarded the Jewish people as a race; because he proposed that Jews be treated as foreign nationals and as citizens of a Jewish state to be founded if they had not lived within the borders of the German Empire before 1 July 1871, or if their ancestors had not lived within the borders of the German Empire before 1 July 1871.[19]

Some of Goerdeler's positions and views have become questionable through the horrors of Auschwitz and all it stands for. Some are contradictory. Goerdeler's suggestion, in a memorandum written in 1941, after years of injustices and cruelties committed by German authorities against German and non-German Jews, to deprive naturalized German Jews of their citizenship, appears shockingly insensitive[20]. Jews in all parts of the world, at least those who were not Zionists, had to see the implications as threatening. But Goerdeler's motive was to secure the Jews' status against future persecution.

Goldhagen ignored the fact that Goerdeler condemned the National Socialists comprehensively because they had "overthrown God with their racial madness"[21], and the fact that Britain controlled Jewish immigration to Palestine.

Goerdeler eventually resigned as Mayor because of the National Socialist anti-Jewish policies. He chose to resign over the removal of the statue outside the Leipzig *Gewandhaus* (Great Concert Hall), which had been erected in 1892 in honour of its former director, Felix Mendelssohn-Bartholdy, rather than on the issue of the public communal baths. He could certainly expect a greater impact from the Mendelssohn statue affair. For years, and most urgently in the spring of 1936, before the summer Olympiad in Berlin, local Party leaders, the new National-Socialist Deputy Mayor, and the City Treasurer pressed the Mayor to permit the removal of the statue. Goerdeler said no. He accepted that the question might be discussed. But he postponed discussion of it indefinitely until after the summer, without setting a date.

In the autumn of 1936 Goerdeler followed an invitation of the German Chamber of Commerce to travel to Helsingfors in Finland. Before he left, he secured Goebbels' and Hitler's approval for his decision to leave the monument where it was, and he instructed Deputy Mayor Haake accordingly. But on 9 November 1936, while Goerdeler was out of town, Haake had the statue removed. Goerdeler demanded an explanation; Haake accused him in a written deposition of 16 November 1936 of not sharing the Party's view on the Jews; of having resisted from 1933 every single re-naming of a street that bore the name of a Jew; and of having obstructed every effort to remove the Mendelssohn-Bartholdy statue. On 25 November 1936 Goerdeler resigned as Mayor. Haake, in a meeting with the City Counsellors on 2 December 1936, declared that the matter of the statue was "only the outward occasion of the conflict", and that "the real cause lay in Dr. Goerdeler's world-view which was the opposite of National Socialism". In a statement of 4 December justifying the City's acceptance of Goerdeler's resignation, Haake said that Goerdeler had criticized and opposed most National Socialist policies since 1933, and that "Dr. Goerdeler's attitude in the Jewish Question had been revealed particularly clearly in the matter of the Mendelssohn-Bartholdy statue"[22].

While the circumstances of Goerdeler's resignation, viewed in isolation, might suggest that the issue of National Socialist anti-Jewish policies was secondary to the issue of his executive authority, this would be misleading. Haake's indictment of Goerdeler in 1936 made this clear. Nor did Goerdeler cease in his resistance to National Socialist racial policies after his resignation.

In a memorandum of 1 December 1937 intended for publication in America, Goerdeler said he was disturbed by the equanimity with which many outside Germany received the news of the Hitler regime's atrocities.[23] At the request of the Head of the British Foreign Office, Sir Robert Vansittart, A. P. Young met with Goerdeler on 6 and 7 August 1938 in Rauschen Dune. Months before the November 1938 pogrom, Goerdeler urged the British government through Young and Vansittart to express their disgust at the National Socialist methods more forcefully, and he urged them to refuse to discuss the vital issues Germany was interested in if the practices against the Jews continued. In a further meeting with A. P. Young, in Switzerland on 6 and 7 November 1938, after some 10,000 Polish Jews had been driven across the German frontier with Poland, three days before the pogrom, Goerdeler predicted "a great increase in the persecution of the Jews and Christians". At the same meeting, he was "greatly perturbed that there is not yet in evidence any strong reaction throughout the democracies, in the Press, the Church, and in Parliament, against the barbaric, sadistic and cruel persecution of 10,000 Polish Jews in Germany".

In information provided to A. P. Young between 4 December 1938 and 15 January 1939, Goerdeler again deplored "the cruel and senseless persecution of the Jews" and "the way in which the Nazi leaders enriched themselves by stealing Jewish property". He warned that Hitler was determined to conquer the world, and that for this purpose he had "decided to destroy the Jews — Christianity — Capitalism". Goerdeler urged the British government to apply strong pressure against Hitler's government "to save the world from this terrible catastrophe". When Goerdeler met A. P. Young on 16 March 1939, the day after the occupation of Czechia by German troops, Goerdeler "was emphatic in his view that Hitler is now on the wrong path" which would lead to his destruction — if the democracies moved swiftly. Goerdeler listed "three milestones of great historical importance" which Hitler had already passed on this path, and he declared the first such milestone to be "The Pogrom against the Jews on November 9 and 10". Goerdeler described this pogrom to A. P. Young as having been ordered by Hitler, and he "spoke with burning indignation", especially of how little children were driven from their homes in the night, and of how young Nazi gangsters violated Jewish virgins.[24]

Although the persecution of the Jews did not motivate Goerdeler exclusively — there were also the mentally ill, after 1 September 1939 the Poles, after 22 June 1941 the Russian prisoners-of-war and civilians, the excessive executions of hostages in France and in the east, all the perversions of justice, and the war itself — the persecution of the Jews received Goerdeler's strongest expressions of condemnation. Goerdeler also felt — it was not the only time he chose his words infelicitously — that it was necessary to point out "the great guilt of the Jews who had intruded themselves into our public life in ways which lacked all appropriate consideration", and almost in the same breath he declared: "And I am not an anti-Semite."

In his "Thoughts of One Condemned to Death about the German Future", written in the days after he had been sentenced in September 1944, Goerdeler stated that Hitler's hands were "dripping with the blood of innocent Jews, Poles, Russians and Germans who were murdered and starved to death, with the blood of millions of soldiers of all nations who are on his conscience". And: "We must not deny the Jews the rights which God gave to all humans." The Secret State Police reported that

Goerdeler, in prison after 20 July 1944, "again and again expressed his outrage about the great massacres of Jews in Poland". He justified his leadership in the conspiracy against the National Socialists as the attempt to liberate the world of "those monsters who sought to upset all values and who elevated the fatherland to a moloch, who had dethroned God with their racial madness". He declared that one must not allow the Germans to cover up what had happened, that around a million of German Jews and an unknown number of Polish and Russian Jews had been "murdered with a bestiality unheard of in world history".[25]

V.

Goldhagen's "expert" told him that there were anti-Jewish attitudes in the Stauffenberg family. His "expert", of course, ignored Alexander Count Stauffenberg's marriage to a woman of Jewish origin, or Berthold Count Stauffenberg's unequivocal condemnation of the persecution of the Jews. During the war Berthold Stauffenberg said to co-workers in Naval High Command that those responsible for crimes "such as concentration camps, persecution of the Jews" must be punished *before* Germany's total military defeat, and that no sacrifice was too great to accomplish that punishment.[26] After the failed uprising of July 1944, Berthold Stauffenberg told his interrogators, speaking also for his brother Claus, that they had approved of the leader principle, of support for agriculture, and of the racial principle, but: "The fundamental ideas of National Socialism have in practice all been perverted into their opposites."[27] There is also some evidence that before 1938 Claus Stauffenberg approved of restrictions upon the Jews in various professions and in the civil service.[28]

When Major (GS) Claus Count Stauffenberg learned of the mass-murder of "racially inferior" persons, especially Jews, he responded that Hitler must be removed. An important point for Claus Stauffenberg's motivation to oppose Hitler is that when between 26 and 30 April 1942 Stauffenberg condemned Hitler's genocidal policies and called for Hitler's overthrow, he still accepted Hitler's military leadership, and he did not consider the war lost. The military professional verdict against Hitler came only later, in July 1942, because Hitler gave directives that led to the Stalingrad desaster.[29]

It was *not*, therefore, the prospect of Germany losing the war that motivated Stauffenberg to attempt the assassination of his supreme commander, but rather the crimes of the regime. A "Proclamation to the Armed Forces" which Stauffenberg prepared with Brigadier Henning von

Tresckow and General Ludwig Beck said:

> We must act because — this weighs most heavily — crimes have
> been committed behind your backs which besmirch the honour
> of the German nation and soil its good name in the world.[30]

The notion that an officer who valued his honor would attempt to
attack his supreme commander because the war was not going well was
foreign to Stauffenberg's and his fellow-officers' thinking. German officers did not rebel because they were not winning. What they could not
accept was that they were being used to cover crimes and dishonour.
Stauffenberg gave this explanation on several occasions in 1943, and so
did Tresckow: It was not that the war was not going well, military service
was after all the tradition in his family; but it was the knowledge that
tens of thousands of Jews were being killed, and it was this above all that
had motivated him and his fellow-plotters to plan the insurrection against
Hitler.[31]

In consequence of his knowledge and conclusions, well before the
Stalingrad catastrophe, and well before he considered the war lost, in the
summer and early autumn of 1942, Stauffenberg *acted, alone*. He approached half a dozen front-line commanders to try to persuade them to
overthrow Hitler, without success.[32]

vi.

The records, which survive incompletely, show that at least fifteen mem-
bers of the anti-Hitler conspiracy stated in interrogations by
Secret-State-Police officers after the failed coup d'état of 20 July 1944,
that their main motive, or, that one of their main motives for their oppo-
sition to National Socialism was the persecution of the Jews: Klaus
Bonhoeffer, Wilhelm Canaris, Hans von Dohnanyi, Carl Goerdeler, Franz
Kempner, Hans Kloos, Adolf Lampe, Heinrich Count Lehndorff-Steinort,
Hans Oster, Alexis Baron von Roenne, Rüdiger Schleicher, Franz Sperr,
Alexander Count Stauffenberg, Berthold Count Stauffenberg, Peter
Count Yorck von Wartenburg. (All except Kloos, Lampe and Alexander
Stauffenberg were executed.)

Twenty-two other anti-Hitler plotters are on record as having been
equally motivated: General Ludwig Beck, Dietrich Bonhoeffer, Major
Axel Baron von dem Bussche, Constantin von Dietze, Eberhard Finckh,
Rudolf-Christoph Baron von Gersdorff, Eugen Gerstenmaier, Carl

Goerdeler, Helmuth Groscurth, Hans-Bernd von Haeften, Ulrich von Hassell, Julius Leber, Carlo Mierendorff, Helmuth James Count Moltke, Johannes Popitz, Adolf Reichwein, Ulrich Count Schwerin von Schwanenfeld, Wilhelm Staehle, Claus Count Stauffenberg, Theodor Steltzer, Helmuth Stieff, Henning von Tresckow, Adam von Trott zu Solz, Josef Wirmer (all executed except Beck and Tresckow who committed suicide; Bussche, Dietze, Gersdorff, Steltzer and Gerstenmaier who survived; Groscurth who died a prisoner-of-war, Mierendorff who was killed in an air raid). There were also a number of Catholic priests and Lutheran ministers, and twenty-eight members of the White Rose student group who made the same declaration.[33]

Hitler's few opponents in Germany were unable to intervene against the mass extermination of the Jews, even though they rescued a few. This is part of the tragedy of the German resistance, because many of Hitler's opponents in Germany were motivated by the persecution of the Jews above all other considerations.

If the critics were right who say that Hitler's German opponents were as anti-Semitic as the rest of German society and therefore co-responsible for "Auschwitz", and that they objected to anti-Jewish policies only when such policies were pursued with "rioting and force"[34], their reference to anti-Jewish outrages and mass-murder as arguments in the struggle against Hitler would have been singularly unsuited to win over confederates. But Bonhoeffer, Dohnanyi, Oster, Tresckow, Beck and Stauffenberg used these references to convince potential military allies to try to obstruct the deportations and atrocities, and to speed the preparations for the overthrow of National Socialism.[35] The fact that these references were made constantly (but not exclusively) in the search for supporters of Hitler's overthrow means that the persecution of the Jews was a fundamental issue for the resistance.

It was not in the arrested resisters' interest to hurl their outrage at the Nazis' crimes against the Jews at their interrogators and torturers; yet many of them did just that. Some combined their condemnations of the regime's actions with the concession that they had initially greeted the National Socialists with approval; others honestly revealed their personal anti-Jewish bias while condemning the regime's crimes. On the other hand, some of the interrogators endeavored to help their charges in exchange for exculpatory affidavits after the Allied victory.[36] Given that there was much that was suppressed or bent to suit the situation, the comprehensive conclusion the Gestapo reached and submitted to Hitler is the more remarkable.

Scholars Answer Goldhagen

The summary of the Secret-State-Police investigation on this subject, written at the end of October 1944, after more than three months of cruel interrogations and torture of approximately seven hundred persons arrested in connection with the conspiracy, reached a shattering conclusion: After three months of intensive investigations, the Gestapo reported (28 October 1944):

> The entire inner alienation from the ideas of National Socialism which characterised the men of the reactionary conspiratorial circle expresses itself above all in their position on the Jewish Question. [...] they stubbornly take the liberal position of granting to the Jews in principle the same status as to every German.

· *Chapter 7* ·

Goldhagen — Another Kind of Revisionism

Erich Geldbach

· 7 ·

Goldhagen — Another Kind of Revisionism

Erich Geldbach

Any comment or even criticism of Daniel Goldhagen's book, *Hitler's Willing Executioners: Ordinary Germans and the Holocaust* by a German will easily sound apologetic. It seems in order, therefore, first of all to say that the book calls to the attention of any decent human being the fact that within Christendom, and especially within Protestant Christendom in Germany, the Jews were forsaken. When the German people, in their political naivete, entrusted their political future to the political terrorists and vandals — although not by a majority as Goldhagen implies, they plunged the country into its severest crisis. As in almost any time of crisis in the past, the Jews again served as scapegoats for every conceivable evil. Anyone who has ever exposed him/herself to the plight of the Jews during the Nazi period, anyone who has ever been touched by accounts of eye-witnesses who were terrorized in the "kingdom of barbed wire", anyone who has ever read detailed descriptions of people who were senselessly brutalized and murdered for no other reason than that they happened to be born Jews, will inevitably be haunted by the question why all this happened. Why did university-educated as well as "ordinary" people turn into killers? Why?!

Clearly, Goldhagen is obsessed by that question — and rightly so. It shows that the subject matter is so sensitive and overwhelming that a "disinterested," "scientific," "objective" encounter is impossible, Since the subject breaks all laws which ordinarily govern our lives, the investigation of necessity must be different from all other "scholarly" or "scientific" studies. Goldhagen cannot be criticized on account of his personal involvement or, as some German critics have done, on account of his father's experience. Any study of aspects of the Holocaust must follow the pattern Goldhagen has chosen. Without a deep personal commitment, Holocaust studies become shallow and fail to produce in the reader the only adequate response, i.e. to work toward the goal that nothing like it will ever happen again in human history.

For this service, Goldhagen deserves to be thanked. The detailed case studies on the Police Battalion 101, on the "work" camps and on the death marches during the last days of the war are presented with all the accompanying horror and with great linguistic skill. It would be hard for any reader not to be immediately affected. These case studies are presented as a partial answer to the agonizing question why ordinary men — and sometimes women — behaved with uncalled for cruelty and turned into willing and even enthusiastic killers of Jewish men, women and even children and babies. Without these ordinary Germans, there would have been no Holocaust. Why did they forget all ethical norms... or did they not?

According to Goldhagen they did not. The likelihood for ordinary Germans to turn into mass killers existed long before the Nazis came to power. Hitler and his inner circle only had to tap a "disastrous potentiality" (p. 15) within the soul of the German people for the Holocaust to take place. The "central intellectual problem for understanding" Nazi Germany (p. 4) can be solved if that potential finds an explanation.

It is obvious from the outset that Goldhagen's approach is centered around the necessity "to explain how Germans came to be such potential willing mass killers". It is also obvious that Goldhagen's attempt to explain this potentiality is guided by the notion that there is "no universality of our common sense". He calls this notion "anthropologically and social-scientifically primitive". The scholar must rid him/herself of the thought that there exist ethical norms that were violated in the case of the mass slaughter of Jews by Germans. For Germans were different from any other European nationals — and presumably not only from other Europeans, but beyond — so that whatever applies anywhere else does not apply in Germany.

Germany is, to Goldhagen, not a "normal" society. Instead he looks at Germany "with the critical eye of an anthropologist disembarking on unknown shores, open to meeting a radically different culture" (p. 15) that pursues its collective products and projects according to very different norms from what would "normally" be the case. Normally one would think that people would have to be forced against their will to perform such evil tasks as to shoot or massmurder innocent babies and children, defenseless mothers and fathers, harmless grandmothers and grandfathers. The normalcy pushed aside, however, reveals that Germans killed Jews in "good conscience". They were not themselves victims of an illegitimate government which followed an unscrupulous policy and had to compel its people to follow orders. Instead Germans wholeheartedly agreed to participate not only willingly but enthusiastically in the "national project" to eliminate the Jews, Goldhagen's main thesis is that Germans acted "normally" when they killed Jews. No ethical obstacles had to be overcome since there were no such restraints. This does not mean that Germans were not aware that human beings should not be killed. Despite numerous killings that occurred in the POW camps among Russian soldiers, Poles or other members of Slavic societies, it is nevertheless true that Jews were especially targeted as the victims of atrocities. This is undeniable and not one of Goldhagen's new insights. It is also uncontested, even though German apologetics after World War II questioned it for a long time, that there were many more Germans involved in the implementation of the anti-Jewish program and that their "willingness" to participate was more forthright than Germans are generally prepared to admit. There can also be no doubt that millions must have known about the mass killings. When confronted with these facts, one can easily understand Goldhagen's search for an answer that would catapult German society into a unique position: Only *here* could the Holocaust have happened. What is new in Goldhagen's book, then, is his contention that in no country other than Germany were people so conditioned against the Jews by a long tradition of hatred of the Jews that it seemed only "natural" to ordinary Germans to "exterminate" European Jewry.

What was the driving force behind this willingness to kill Jews in good conscience and "for pleasure" (p. 451)? The answer for Goldhagen is as clear as can be. It was the age-old antisemitism which moved hundreds of thousands of willing German perpetrators to dehumanize and slaughter six million Jews, and antisemitism would have moved millions more Germans had they been given a chance to participate in this national project. Goldhagen dismisses any other factor that may have contributed to motivate Germans to act as they did: "Not economic hardship, not the coercive means of a totalitarian state, not social psychological pressure, not invariable psychological propensities, but ideas about Jews that were pervasive in Germany, and had been for decades, induced ordinary Germans to kill... systematically and without pity" (p. 9). The "extermination" of the Jews was in accordance with these German "ideas about Jews" and was right. A minority of Germans may have consulted their conscience and may have chosen not to kill, but the behavior of the "vast majority" of Germans was governed by their zeal to kill. There was no need for them to say no. In fact, they greatly enjoyed what they were doing, "had fun" (p. 235) and did their job with pride.

Antisemitism, it must be assumed, could not possibly have been the only motive for the Germans to commit their atrocities, for antisemitism is a highly complex phenomenon and in no way limited to Germany. Although his use of the term "antisemitism" leaves much to be desired, Goldhagen of course knows that Germany was not the only country where "negative beliefs and emotions about Jews *qua* Jews" — so the inadequate definition (p. 34) — existed. Therefore he argues that German antisemitism was of a special kind. It was radically different from any other variety of antisemitism -Russian, Polish, Lithuanian, French, let alone Danish or Italian. "The notion that ordinary Danes or Italians would have acted as the ordinary Germans did strains credulity beyond the breaking point" (p. 408).

What was it, however, that made German antisemitism so unique among the various forms of antisemitism? It is Goldhagen's claim to have found the answer, an answer which is "new to the scholarly literature" or even "stands in contradiction to the existing literature" (see p. 480, n. 33). Not only is Goldhagen's answer new and revolutionary, but, as he ascribes these qualities to it, it must also be considered the hermeneutical key to understanding Goldhagen's whole book. The Germans are distinguished from any other nation in that they carried the Christian antisemitism of the Middle Ages continuously to the 19th century, mixed or replaced it with social Darwinism and the concept of "race" to make it appear "scientific," and passed it on to the 20th century.

Antisemitism was a continuing axiom of German culture, more or less dormant or manifest, but always present as a central individual and collective feature (p. 45). Since the notion that the Germans were "neutral" toward the Jews presents a "psychological impossibility" to explain the atrocities during the Nazi period, their socially transmitted thoughts and feelings about the Jews must be the source of German brutality (p. 481, n. 43). These thoughts and feelings made up the typically German belief system, the "cognitive model" about the Jews (p. 46).

Antisemitism is thus established by Goldhagen as "endemic to German culture and society". It is so endemic that antisemitism exerted "a magical spell" on the Germans: Germans were obsessed with the Jews. The "Jewish question" became Germany's primary phobia.

As one would expect if a phobia is diagnosed, there needs to be a way to rectify the abnormal situation. So it is with Goldhagen's theory: German antisemitism is characterized by an element which the author calls "eliminationist". German society was for centuries and decades inundated by the urge to get rid of the Jews. To be sure, this does not necessarily mean that Jews needed to be killed. Other means were also being discussed in the German culture. However, the "eliminationist" kind of antisemitism had the upper hand and permeated German society to such an extent that it became the "normal" way of thinking about Jews.

Eliminationist antisemitism became the "common sense" and was "extremely widespread in all social classes and sectors of German society" (p. 77). It was this ideology which had been culturally transmitted as the cognitive model of the Jews that was at the root of the policies which the Nazis implemented and which the ordinary Germans eagerly and willfully accepted and supported (see p. 127). They were far from expressing any dissent to the Jewish policy of the Nazis because that policy was not alien to their own thoughts and feelings. Germans were driven by their desire to eliminate all Jewish influence from society (p. 48). Thus the answer which the Nazi leadership provided to the "Jewish question" coincided with the endemic and long-inherited and therefore "culturally ubiquitous" eliminationist antisemitism. To mobilize ordinary Germans to kill Jews with pleasure was an easy task for propaganda: from "eliminationist antisemitism" to the Nazi extermination program is but a very small step.

On the surface, the catch-phrase "no Germans, no Holocaust" is true. But just as the models of that phrase — "no bishop, no king" or "no bishop, no church" — echoed the prevailing theory of the time, there were, nevertheless, quite a number (although difficult to assess how many) of non-conforming dissidents who at that time preferred to believe in "no cross, no crown", as did William Penn. There can be no doubt that not enough courageous German men and women were willing to risk their lives to obtain the "crown of life", but there can equally be no doubt that there were some, perhaps more than under the prevailing circumstances will ever be known, who did not bow their knees to Baal.

There is enough evidence to suggest that ideological factors were primary in motivating Germans to kill not only Jews, but also Sinti and Roma, also members of Slavic nations as "subhumans" and the mentally disabled as "worthless". Nowhere does Goldhagen entertain the thought that the ideology could have been acquired under the extremely effective Nazi propaganda and indoctrination machinery. According to Goldhagen's view not only the disposition, but also the thoughts and feelings, were socially transmitted and therefore acquired well before the Nazis came to power. He excludes any factors other than antisemitism: it constitutes his only explanation. Antisemitism is not one among some or many factors, but the sole explanatory cause for the Holocaust. Germans had just waited for their golden opportunity to kill.

In a bizarre reversal of the Nazi's conception of "the" Jew, Goldhagen sees the national soul of "the" Germans infected by the virus of antisemitism. The multiple redundancy of Goldhagen's presentation of this axiomatic thesis does not make his claim any more convincing than his dismissal of all previous literature on the subject, or his presupposition that Germany was like an "unknown" shore of an as yet undiscovered island. His monocausal explanation is not only simplistic: it actually decontextualizes the Holocaust — so much so that "*the* Germans" are mythologized. They become "demons" (which the perpetrators undoubtedly were, especially in the eyes of the victims) in their obsessive attempt to make Europe "judenfrei". The Holocaust carried German antisemitism to its logical end and thus became a historic necessity. The "demons" murdered the "metaphysical enemies".

If German antisemitism was indeed unique, it would be necessary to make a comparison with other forms of antisemitism in France or Poland, in the Ukraine or Russia, in Latvia or Lithuania to provide evidence of a German *"Sonderweg"* ("special case"). Goldhagen dismisses such a comparative approach with the unconvincing argument that the facts speak for themselves and that the burden of proof rests with those who oppose his view. This is neither methodologically sound nor is it analytically a step in the right direction. It only shows Goldhagen's axiomatic purpose.

The argument goes in circles. Because the Holocaust was a unique event, the perpetrators must have been driven by a unique motive. As the only motive was antisemitism, it must have been a unique form. No unique form of German antisemitism, no Holocaust. As antisemitism was "ubiquitous" and had affected all sectors of German society, the sociological axiom serves as the causal model. The perpetrators were normal Germans, as exemplified by the Police Battalions. Hence all normal Germans are perpetrators, actually or virtually. Hence all Germans are potential little Eichmanns, and therefore "abnormal" by "normal" criteria.

Even though Goldhagen never expressly uses the term "collective guilt," he comes very close to embracing this theory (see p. 499 n. 30 where he quotes approvingly a "German Jewish Scientist" who had escaped early), except that his version of "collective guilt" may turn out to be far more dangerous than when that theory was first applied to Germany after World War I. For Goldhagen's theory disallows all possibility to hold people morally responsible for their acts. "The Germans" could not act any other way: they were predestined by their generations-long exposure to "eliminationist antisemitism" to act as they did.

On another level, one may examine whether it is legitimate to draw as wide-ranging conclusions as Goldhagen does. Even though the example may seem to be very trivial, the question can, nevertheless, be asked whether the urge of soldiers to kill allows us to make generalizations about the individual aggressive character or that of his battalion, group or even his nation. Is it justifiable to conclude that all Americans are brutal because my defenseless, unarmed mother was attacked by an American airman from a low-flying military airplane early in 1945 as she was riding her bicycle from the village where she had taken her household to the town where she had left the house and store unattended? Clearly, such a generalization would be out of order and of course the incident does not come even close to the crimes that were committed against the Jews. But if several hundred thousand — or a million -Germans were involved in the "extermination" program — and it is highly probable that Goldhagen is right in assessing the number much higher than had previously been assumed, does this justify expanding that number to include all "the Germans"?

Who is "a German?" Are Austrians included? Not only Hitler himself, but also Eichmann, Kaltenbrunner and other high officials came from Austria. It is estimated that one third of the SS units which were used in the "extermination" campaign came from Austria. Are Luxemburgers included? There were some who served in the Police Battalion which Goldhagen investigated. Are Romanians of German descent or other *Volksdeutsche* (ethnic Germans outside the homeland) included? They are said to have been especially brutal. And what was the role of Ukrainians, Latvians, Lithuanians who assisted? Did not even Dutch and French collaborators round up Jews in order for them to be sent to the concentration camps?

It also appears that Adolf Hitler and other Nazi officials were not as sure of the ubiquity of antisemitism in German society as is Goldhagen, for the government and its propaganda machinery as well as its surveillance organizations took many precautionary steps to keep the "extermination" program as much a secret as possible and to monitor the people and their attitudes. To repeat: more Germans must have known, more must have been involved, and more must have liked what they saw and did. Goldhagen deserves credit for calling our attention to these facts. But why does Goldhagen time and again use his favorite term "vast majority" (e.g. pp. 8, 56, 87, 88, 90, 102, etc.) of Germans or simply "the Germans"? How can the "vastness" be determined, especially if this idea of vastness is projected back into the past and applied to a 150-year history? Which criteria can methodologically be used to find out what the "vast" majority of Germans was "thinking and feeling"? Is it legitimate to concentrate on eccentric, sometimes even pathological figures (viz Graf Pückler) and their writings or simply on the "corpus of German antisemitic literature" (p. 28) and to draw from that the matter-of-fact conclusion that such were the views "dominant throughout German society" (p. 55)? How does one measure "dominant"?

One also wonders how amidst the "eliminationist antisemitism" the emancipation and assimilation of the Jews could have taken place or why Jews would then stay in Germany and make invaluable contributions to the economic, medical, theatrical, journalistic and cultural life of the country. Why would they consider this "deeply antisemitic culture" their own fatherland? If "the Germans" were eager to eliminate them, were all of them living under an illusion? Goldhagen would probably answer that these Jews may have encountered Germans in whom antisemitism was "dormant" at the time. This dormancy is another of his presuppositions. Overt antisemitism is not needed to make a society antisemitic. It may for a while be "dormant," only to erupt with brutal force again. It is undoubtedly true that there is antisemitism even without Jews, and it may also be true that antisemitism comes and goes in waves. What is implied, however, is a far-reaching problem for post-war Germany, as several critics have pointed out.

If Goldhagen is correct that German society was deeply infected by antisemitism and that antisemitism may be latent for a while, where did it go in 1945? All sectors of German society could not have so easily purged themselves of this infectious disease so as to make it evaporate within a few hours. To be sure, after the war there were very few who honestly confessed to having been Nazis and antisemites. Most people claimed to have been victims or *Mitläufer* ("fellow-travelers"). That this was but a cheap excuse is evident. Then, however, the question what happened to the German antiseptic *Sonderweg* ("special case") becomes so much more important. Has German antisemitism been "dormant" for the last few decades, and is there the ever present danger that it may erupt again? Is the "new" Germany after unification especially in danger of becoming, once again, the seed-bed of antisemitism of the exterminationist type? Will German antisemitism again show its ugly face in a time of economic or social crisis? Can "the Germans" be trusted

Hyping the Holocaust

as the twenty-first century approaches??

Antisemitism — however defined, and Goldhagen uses the term very floatingly — is far more international in scope than Goldhagen presents it. The international Congresses of Antisemites at the end of the 19th century and well into the 20th century were attended by many Germans, but also by "delegates" from other countries such as Hungary, Romania, Russia, France, Great Britain, etc. One Congress even took place in Denmark. On the other hand the only identifiable groups in Germany which held no antisemitic views were not "small" groups, as Goldhagen contends. The socialists and the left-liberals were very large in comparison to antisemitic parties which were, in fact, very small as political entities. The notion that in the election of 1893 the Reichstag had an "avowedly antisemitic" majority (p. 75) is pure fiction. There were sixteen deputies who had been elected as members of antisemitic parties which is roughly 5% of the popular vote.

There is no doubt that antisemitism in Germany was widespread and, as Goldhagen sees it, more so than generally admitted. It is also incontestable that it played the major role in the Nazi campaign to make the world "judenrein". However, Goldhagen's monocausal "explanation" of the Holocaust which amounts to a new and far more radical "intentionalist" theory is also incompatible with the findings of the "functionalist" school. Whatever its deficits are, it seems well established that the Holocaust occurred as an unfolding drama. It is "multi-causal" and developed in stages, and the last stage — the so-called "final solution" — took place under the conditions of an all-out war and after a period of several years in which people had been subject to an exceptionally sophisticated propaganda system of a dictatorship. To eliminate these situational factors is highly questionable. It may also be questioned whether there was, in fact, "substantial freedom and pluralism" (p. 479 n. 32) in Nazi German society, Even if this were so and even if the dictatorship was not as monolithic as it is often portrayed, the degree of voluntarism with which Germans killed still says very little. As can be gathered by a less severe case of dictatorship like the former German Democratic Republic, a regime can produce hundreds of meters of reports of disagreement with, opposition to, or discontent with a great many areas of life, which on the surface could be interpreted as a sign of "substantial freedom" or of a high degree of voluntarism. Yet this says little or nothing with regard to the actual ability of people to change the course of things.

One of the accompanying dangers, although, of course, not intended by the author, is the reaction the book has caused among the conservatives and nationalists. One example may be Peter Gauweiler, the head of the Christian Social Union (CSU) in Munich. In the party's organ, *Bayernkurier*, he simply dismissed the book and concluded that there could not have been more than 50,000 Germans who "knew" about the Holocaust at the time it happened. Goldhagen's explanatory oversimplification makes it easy for die-hards *not* to face the issues which the Holocaust presents and with which he rightly would like his readers to be confronted.

The book does confront the reader with an enormous amount of questions. The case studies, presented in clear language and with all the brutal facts, raise issues of a magnitude that correlates to the *SHOA* as a "watershed event" (so F. H. Littell) in human history. Goldhagen's attempt to "explain" what happened says more about his own socialization and context than about the context of the Holocaust.

Goldhagen grew up in American society at a time when a simple reductionism was promulgated by the top man in the White House. Ronald Reagan used the language pattern which Goldhagen also utilizes: "They" are not "like us"- "they" are not the children of enlightenment as "we are". Similarly, there is no similarity between "us" and "Germans": "the Germans" operate on a different "common sense". "They" are not only part of an "evil empire", they are the very representatives of the evil empire. Whereas it is true that Germany of the Nazi period was an evil empire, and whereas it is equally true that Germans need to be reminded of their past, it is, at the same time imperative that such an admonition be done so as not to become counter-productive. Goldhagen's simplistic reductionism will not have healing effects, It will strengthen those in Germany who despite all the evidence are now less inclined to listen; it will give other nations with antisemitic traditions an easy way out; and it will drive a wedge between the USA, Germany and Israel as countries immediately concerned. It will possibly also ignite new forms of antisemitism.

Goldhagen made an attempt to speak the unspeakable. He is right to speak up because men and women of conscience dare not be silent. Silence is complicity with those who experimented with a genocidal operation as a means of social engineering, and with those who became "willing executioners" of such plans. Without University-educated men and women as well as without "normal" people, the Holocaust would have been impossible. Because it was a break-down of civilization, there must never be a *"Schlusstrich"*-mentality (the idea "to close the books") in Germany or elsewhere. The language which is being used, the paradigms which are being presented, must be such that generations to come will be in a position to remember.

Goldhagen's reductionism is coupled with a "we — they" dichotomy which also implies a superior moralistic attitude. His over-inflated claim to originality goes hand in glove with his self-declared contention to present *the* breakthrough in Holocaust studies — as though this field were the right opportunity for one's self-aggrandizement. These factors may turn out to be counter-productive, for they make him and his book vulnerable to a degree that neither the subject-matter nor Goldhagen deserve.

· Chapter 8 ·

In Reaction to
Daniel Goldhagen's Book

Wolfgang Gerlach

· 8 ·

In Reaction to Daniel Goldhagen's Book

Wolfgang Gerlach

In evaluating the Goldhagen book I find myself in a remarkable conflict. Twenty five years ago Christian publishers were warned by theological appraisers not to publish my dissertation on "The Confessing Church and the Third Reich." The reason: my work was irresponsible. For I had demolished the picture of a church that claimed to have withstood all and everything through confession of faith, and I had made specific the guilt to which this church had confessed in Stuttgart, 1945, so openly if also abstractly.

And now, today, I read this book by Goldhagen with discontent similar to that of my critics then. The few in the church who took both theological and practical risks for the Jews — not seldom at risk of their professional existence or life itself — we want to appear today as an important minority who deserve to be named and not suppressed. And all the more so because Goldhagen's satanizing of *the* Germans reminds me clearly of the caricature of *the* Jews by the antisemites of the Nazi era.

I cannot recall when it was so difficult for me to review a book. An intellectual as well as emotional discontent grows throughout, as the author announces precision in a substantive analysis as in the following evaluation, and the reader instead confronts a fog of generalizations, demonizing, a poverty of differentiation between concepts. Beyond that there is an indifference about the necessity of appropriately evaluating the behavior and the citing of "perpetrators" in respect to their place in time. In place of the anatomy of antisemitism and a description of its consequences we have a moralistic provocation and emotional pillorizing:

> "The moral bankruptcy of the German churches, Protestant and Catholic alike, regarding Jews was so extensive and abject that it warrants far more attention than can be devoted to it here." (p. 107)

I will limit myself in the main to those passages in Goldhagen's book dealing with the church — that is, the churches in Germany — and their reaction in respect to the laws and the treatment of the Jews by the National Socialists. It is precisely in this area that Goldhagen refers to my research and the sources I collected, but he constantly applies them quite differently. At first glance I see two reasons for this. First, one familiar with the materials gets the impression that Goldhagen is not familiar enough with the German church relations and structures, their historical developments and their variety of aspects, to achieve a reliable assessment. Second, his view here and at other places is driven or directed by the "research" conclusion with which he starts, that German antisemitism (that is, not just antisemitism in Germany) has been to its deepest roots "eliminationist antisemitism" — also in the church as well as in its prominent representatives.

It is as though Goldhagen photographs the intellectual and cultural landscape of Germany from a great distance, which makes it impossible for him to organize and evaluate the in some respects notable historical and theological differences. In this he is lacking a "zoomer" to draw the distant scene near, which would give clear outlines to the blurred and draw the previously invisible into the picture.

The pamphleteering style, over long passages arousing the feelings more than the understanding, shows itself hardly entitled to claim scientific format, at least so far as that is customary in Europe. Even if on this topic the scientific admonition to distance one's self and adopt a style *sine ira et studio* ("beyond passion and zeal") is especially hard to achieve, every conclusion of Goldhagen nevertheless loses authority when in many places an appeal to sentiment and a moralistic sense takes the place of the documentations and sources that are lacking.

This charge should now be validated in detail.

1. Comments on the Concept of Antisemitism

Goldhagen promises to offer a "new examination of antisemitism" ("recasting the view of antisemitism," p. 27). In this he apparently starts with the assumption that — in spite of some definitions known to everyone — every form of enmity toward Jews and animosity toward Jews is to be called "antisemitic." In my experience and also conviction it has been shown to be helpful to relate the content of that which is antisemitism to the historical appearance of the concept. Thus my understanding of "antisemitism" was grounded in the observation that the enmity toward the Jews which had been present since the beginning of Christianity acquired for the first time in the 19th century a fully new and aggressive dimension through the racist/biological dividing of humanity into racially inferior and superior groups. The ostensible relationship between *Bios* and *Ethos,* ideologically projected, was to reflect a new pattern of genetic, cultural and social division between "Aryans" and "Semites." Thus the orientalist and philosopher Paul de Lagarde — in the racist line of thought of the Frenchman Joseph Gobineau and the Englishman Houston Stewart Chamberlain — drew a picture of Jews which "the poor, drained Germans" are without compassion "to stamp out like vermin." And he passed on to the Nazis the welcome metaphor: "you don't deal with trichina and bacilli;" they are not to be educated either; "as quickly as possible they are to be rendered harmless." That is the language of antisemitic barbarians, from whom the discovery of a superior "Aryan race" and an inferior "Semitic race" derives. Out of it was postulated a hostility toward the Jews, pointed up in a threefold proposition: the Jews are a race; the Jews are inferior; the Jews are a disintegrative factor. Over against them the "Aryan race" declared itself the ruling race, and from that derived the right and the duty to denounce every crossing of Jews with "Aryans" to be a racial damage and disgrace.

This idea, grounded in racism, gave enmity toward the Jews a completely new dimension, never present before. It was the journalist Wilhelm Marr who — in his best-selling book *Der Sieg des Judentums über das Germanentum* ("The Triumph of Jewry over the Germans," 1873) — invented the word "antisemitism" *(Antisemitismus).* A late romantic fuss about being German appeared to be made about manufacturing identity by repudiating everything supposedly foreign. The longing also for a "biological" catharsis in the so-called "German essence" was united with the previously "only" theological or pseudo-theological aversion toward "the" Jews. The Theo-logic of the 1900-year-old anti-Judaism then provided the seedbed for an a-logical antisemitism aimed at stirring up the emotions.

As is well known, the emotional dimension of antisemitism includes all that which the research on prejudice has compiled in the last 50 years, in a quantity scarcely to be mastered. Goldhagen has nothing to add to this either. Antisemitism can be compared to a cancerous growth, the metastasis of which can long flourish in the darkness, until it manifests itself when time is short or consciousness of identity has become problematical, and its destructive effects are demonstrated both individually and collectively. As a prejudice, antisemitism doesn't need Jewry; that is, even if the Christians had eliminated all of the Jews, antisemitism would still live.

This concept could have appeared earlier if the spiritual ground had been suitable. New concepts become possible on the basis of given or arising cultural movements, attitudes, or also social upheaval.

A clear distinction between antisemitism and anti-Judaism seems to me necessary when we read in Goldhagen: "In the middle ages and the early modern period, without question until the Enlightenment, German society was thoroughly antisemitic." (p. 30)

I hold that for a confusion of concepts and also for a distortion of the true historical relationships. For what he means is one of the various levels of the *anti-Judaism* that has penetrated the Germans since the time of education in the New Testament.

2. Comments on the Concept of Anti-Judaism

Even if a *clear differentiation* between the two phenomena of antisemitism and anti-Judaism is debated, I maintain a *clear distinction* to be essential for both historical and theological reasons. If the element of eliminationism is at the core of antisemitism — and here Goldhagen is right — then anti-Judaism has the goal of "theological" cancellation or elimination of the Jewish faith, which is to be "baptized to death."

I think it important to confirm that in such a differentiation I have no intention of rendering anti-Judaism innocuous; particularly — though I think it evident that it did not necessarily lead to the Holocaust — since I think it cannot be denied that it helped make it possible. I hope it doesn't sound cynical when I assert: it is a religious and theological error to want to drive out another's faith by making him a proselyte; it is also an outrage against the Bible to defame the religious conviction of another to the advantage of one's own faith. Thus I hold the phrase "Nulla salus extra ecclesiam," which is still asserted by many Christians and theologians, to be a false doctrine, which is taught frighteningly by a familiar saying in the mouth of the people: "Und willst du nicht mein Bruder sein, so schlag ich dir den Schädel ein." ("And if you won't be my brother, I'll crack your skull!")

Antisemitism as Christian and ecclesiastical enmity toward the Jews is justified theologically by the refusal of the Jewish people to recognize the Jew Jesus of Nazareth as the Christ, that is as the Messiah who has come. Anti-Judaism is thus nourished by the claim of the church to be the single source of salvation. Whoever disputes this offer of salvation through the church alone, or even calls it a mistaken usurpation, proves himself to the church that argues this way to be "impenitent" and a traitor to the salvation made possible through the death and resurrection of Jesus.

While according to the opinion of the anti-Judaists *the* Jews murdered Jesus on the cross the first time, now they kill him a second time by such non-recognition of his healing work and his salvatory act. Anti-Judaism holds fast to the opposition of the "blind synagogue" and the "seeing church," hewn in stone in the Strassburg cathedral, until Jewry is liquidated or drowned through baptism.

Already by the time of the Church Fathers of the 2nd and 3rd centuries a theology had been constructed which perceived the judgment of God in the destruction of the Temple by the Romans (70 C.E.), which damned the "unbelieving" Jews and elevated from baptism the successor to the elect people. The church was then consolidated in the posture of a "victor-religion," and saw itself divinely legitimated (!) to take over the heritage of the Old Israel. From this dogma of disinheritance, which today we can only call usurpationist-imperialistic, the church fell into a theologically based anti-Judaism which in the course of time strongly influenced the thinking and acting, speaking and silence of Christianity.

With his simplistic thesis of "eliminationist antisemitism," which *the* churches also are supposed to have swallowed whole, Goldhagen is just neither to the Confessing Christians nor the individual bishops or pastors in their thinking and action.

Let us look at some of the better known churchmen of the Nazi time, whom Goldhagen has in his gun-sight.

3. A Look at the Churchly Perpetrators

Goldhagen accuses the Protestant church (to the extent that he doesn't simply at once toss it into one pot with the Catholic) and especially its bishops of having been either active or consenting to the elimination of the Jews. From many angles this judgment is either inaccurate or false. A presentation that made distinctions would have had to use the scientific findings that have been available for a long time, which give a picture of the various "camps" in the Protestant church and their positions — the Lutheran German Christians — who granted Hitler messianic qualities; the socalled "intact" territorial churches of Hannover, Württemberg and Bavaria — which in order to maintain themselves steered a modestly distant course from the Nazi state (but occasionally offered the devil a little finger!); the parishes and pastors of reformed (that is, Calvinistic) orientation — which traditionally cultivated a theology friendly to Israel [i.e., the Jewish people] and had a critical position toward the state that was theologically equipped. Immediately, at the beginning of the Church Struggle *(Kirchenkampf)*, this resulted in various groups, working against each other — not least of all in their pronouncements on the introduction of the Aryan Paragraph into the church. Unfortunately, in Goldhagen there is nothing to be read about these highly varied movements. One can only infer that such a differentiated presentation would have inconvenienced or called his basic thesis into question, which cries out: *The Protestant churches have participated actively or as spectators in the process of the elimination of the Jews, indeed they have consciously cooperated in wiping them out.*

More yet: although the literature from which he frequently cites describes all of these nuances, such observations are tossed aside as unscientific or not useful to the basic pursuit of the Holocaust. Thus he lets slide any notice that — and how — the several churches and parishes distinguished between their attitude to the Jews and to Jewish Christians. And directly a-historical is his writing method, which neglects any historical arrangement of votes, discussions, and decisions. As though it is — or could be -a matter of indifference whether a word hostile to Jews was spoken in 1933 after the boycott of Jewish shops, in 1935 after the Nürnberg Laws, in 1938 after the Night of Broken Glass *(Reichskristallnacht)*, or in 1941 after the start of the first transports to Auschwitz!

Bishop Otto Dibelius. He belonged to the then and — rarely encountered — contemporary opponents of the Jews who have never concealed their antisemitism. (For most deny this position or understand nothing about the latent cancer growing within.) And Goldhagen cites part of a 1928 letter of the former General Superintendent of the Kurmark, where he calls himself an antisemite and expresses his conviction "that in all of the corrosive manifestations of modern civilization Jewry plays a leading role" (p. 109).

On the same page of my book, from which he here cited, he should have recognized and revealed "another Dibelius," where to my 1965 question the bishop responded in writing how his antisemitic position had changed at the time of the persecution of the Jews by the Nazis:

"The situation changed after 1933. That the Protestant Christian stands by the one who is unjustly treated and finally oppressed is self-evident. I have always been happy that I was successful in saving two Jewish families during the whole time of persecution, also at risk of my own freedom."

You can take whatever position about him that you wish. He was not a person who later puts himself in the right light and touches up his photo. Thus there is also the verbal testimony of Dibelius' later assistant, after the war: Eberhard Bethge, who states that about 1941 Dibelius responded spontaneously and decisively to the request for help of Berlin women who were forging underground passes for Jews who wanted to emigrate. Dibelius is a living example of the fact that an antisemite too may involve himself in the rescue of Jews, at risk of his own life.

Dibelius and the not few who responded and acted like him refute the thesis of Goldhagen that "German antisemitism" was "eliminationist" in essence. Dibelius is also an incarnation of that inconsistency which reads as follows: the antisemite in me allows the thorns to grow up in me against the collective Jew; the Christian and human being in me intercedes for him where he is made to suffer. He was not in the situation to resolve this contradiction, because he had not perceived his own contempt for humanity in his antisemitism.

Martin Niemöller. Goldhagen has only read about Niemöller secondhand. (He cites almost exclusively secondary literature.) Goldhagen correctly recognizes that Niemöller could be simultaneously "a committed opponent of the Nazis who was also an antisemite." ("Niemöller serves as an exemplar of the committed anti-Nazi who was a committed antisemite." p. 506) This refutes on the one hand the Goldhagen thesis that the essence of National Socialism consisted of antisemitism, and also the reverse: that German antisemitism was fundamentally shaped by National Socialism. For both there are enough contrary illustrations. There were nationalists who fought the elimination of the Jews; and there were antisemites who like Niemöller were sworn enemies of National Socialism. Goldhagen's single-minded thesis about German antisemitism as "eliminationist" from the beginning is truthfully too simple to withstand more exact testing.

Martin Niemöller, who in the USA is seen exclusively as a personal prisoner of Hitler, enjoys the reputation in the States of being a resister, a friend and rescuer of Jews. Thankfully Goldhagen hasn't settled on these legends. There are too many sayings by this pastor which after the war unconsciously reveal his anti-Judaistic convictions. In contrast to Dibelius, Niemöller had a chance to alter his anti-Judaistic position only until his imprisonment in 1937. The courage which he always showed would presumably driven him to active intervention for persecuted Jews. But late in advanced age it was still not possible for him to perceive how his anti-Judaistic theology was co-responsible for the Holocaust.

Bishop Theophil Wurm. The deeply rooted antisemitism in the Württemberg territorial bishop is correctly described by Goldhagen. And yet he is not fair to him, because he acts as though it was at all times an easy thing to raise a protest against the Nazi extermination politics. Not only at this point is the deficiency of Goldhagen's work evident: he has no idea of the possibilities and the limitations in a totalitarian state of keeping one's conscience pure without compromise, of surviving, and of saving the lives of the persecuted.

Thus there is no mention of the danger in which Bishop Wurm — even if late, too late — in various letters to the Chancellor's office in 1943 protested against the extirpation of the Jews. In his final letter he declared "that we Christians feel this extermination politics against Jewry to be a heavy injustice, ominous for the German nation."

Because Goldhagen sweepingly ascribes "eliminationist" antisemitism to all the church leaders, he denies himself an insight into the varied motives — in, for example, episcopal styles of action. In contrast to Bishop Dibelius, Bishop Wurm first came in 1943 to reflection. And it was not by a direct way that he was let to recognize his antisemitism as an original cause for the murder of the Jews. Rather his eyes were opened to the destruction of the Jews in the moment when in nights of bombing, flight and helplessness "the populace had very painfully to recall what the Jews had to suffer under earlier circumstances." In sum, the Christians in Germany first had to take it in the neck before a bishop comprehended these hardships as God's punishment for the failure to help the persecuted Jews.

Goldhagen suppresses his knowledge of the extremely sharp warning by Minister Lammer to Wurm against his ever again mixing "in questions of public policy." Apparently, the documents imply, his life was saved by a soothing letter from one of his Church Counsellors. Although Goldhagen on one hand never tires of claiming that *the* Germans were in their overwhelming majority saturated by an eliminationist antisemitism and therefore convinced of the necessity of destroying Jewry, he had to indicate in a footnote — that is, hidden — the "camouflaging language rules of the regime," which dictated that the genocide was not to be called what it was in public and even in most official correspondence" (p. 506).

Hyping the Holocaust

In spite of such Nazi politics of camouflage, it appears to Goldhagen "highly unlikely" that between 1941 and 1943 these church people haven't known that mass destruction was hidden behind the exile to the east. "The notion that they were ignorant of the ongoing killing is difficult to accept, given how widespread the knowledge of mass extermination already was." For the church leaders had control of channels of information which "made them often among the best-informed people in the country." This charge has no connection with reality. Even at the time of the Stuttgart Declaration of Guilt in October, 1945 the ecumenical representatives spoke of hundreds of thousands being murdered; abroad too there was no idea of the several millions.

What I can neither acknowledge nor understand is the charge that the Protestant churches for the most part adhered to an antisemitism that ended in the annihilation of the Jews. That seems to me a charge not proven and hard to prove, for which the evidence is not yet available. What can be historically established beyond doubt is the guilt which the church leaders themselves admitted and testified after the war — guilt silenced, made innocuous and with eyes averted, or — since it was too late — not having had the courage or strength to stop the railroad cars rolling toward the gas chambers.

At the international conference in Seattle [at the 14th Annual Scholars' Conference on the Holocaust and the Churches] ("Fifty Years After Barmen," 1984), Bonhoeffer's biographer Eberhard Bethge said: "The Confessing Church resisted by confessing but failed to confess by resisting."

4. Were the Churches "passive"?

The charge of a "striking impassiveness" by both of the large churches in respect to the destruction of the Jews is simply false. ("In sum, in the face of the persecution and annihilation of the Jews, the churches, Protestant and Catholic, as corporate bodies exhibited an apparent, striking impassiveness." p. 437) The truth is rather that the Protestant churches, at least, were trapped and helpless in the cage of their anti-Judaistic tradition.

The stormy, highly controversial discussions of 1933 about the introduction of the Aryan Paragraph in the churches showed the uncertainty and helplessness of the church leaders, university theologians and parishes because of a lacking or distorted theology of the Jewish people. There's nothing to the "passivity" that Goldhagen emphasizes. Admittedly the anti-Judaistic theology in Lutheranism was so strong that the

Reformed (the Calvinists) often stood alone with their theology of love
for the Jewish people. In 1933 the theological debate about the socalled
"Jewish issue" still left open the ecclesiastical line on Jews and socalled
Jewish Christians.

Even if one generally misses in the Protestant press resistance to the
Nazis' policy on the Jews, some individual journals — such as for example the *Breslauer Wochenblatt* — resisted with biting sarcasm. On the
front page there is a provocative "Vision:" Leading the worship service at
the altar, the preacher cries out: "Non-Aryans are requested to leave the
church." This happens three times without anything happening. "Then
Christ stepped down from the cross and left the church." This was still
possible in 1933! But events then took a course about which one could
today say that the ethical dimension was ever and again drowned out by
theological (!) considerations.

That had the result that the famous theological Barmen Declaration
of 1934 left the Jews and also Jewish Christians unmentioned in the six
articles that affirmed and rejected. Karl Barth, the author of these de-
claratory paragraphs later answered a question about this deficit by saying that if he had formulated a 7th article — a so-called "Aryan Paragraph" — the newly welded front of Lutherans and Reformed would
have been ruined. One has to agree with Karl Barth. Anxiety about a
collapse of the newly constituted Confessing Church, in which for the
first time since the Reformation Lutherans and Reformed had agreed
theologically, tempted those responsible at Barmen to be silent about the
distress of Jewish brethren and sisters. For thirty years that has been deeply
mourned in Germany. But from that you cannot argue an eliminationist
antisemitism.

At Steglitz in 1935 the synod was not able to adopt the Memorandum — which Goldhagen also mentions — that "cried out" for the Jews
and Jewish Christians. Question: why does Goldhagen's praise sound
only for the author of the Memorandum, Marga Meusel, and not mini-
mally for the one who made it possible and supported it, Superintendent
Martin Albertz? Does that perhaps not fit the picture of a church which
has to be portrayed as "indolent," as "indifferent?"

One looks in vain in Goldhagen for the few protests and sermon
reactions — which have become generally known — following
Kristallnacht (1938). Unforgettable was Helmut Gollwitzer's sermon on
Repentance Day, in which the listeners well knew how to listen between
the lines for what was intended. For his plain condemnation of the bru-
talities of the Nazis the Swabian pastor Julius von Jan of Oberlenningen

was given heavy beatings after 9 November 1938, lost his parish, and remained a physical wreck. Goldhagen depreciates "the very few, scattered, impassioned, yet barely audible and utterly ineffectual voices of reproach and protest" (p. 437). Thus it can happen that Goldhagen refers to the sermon of the Thuringen bishop Martin Sasse, as rare as it was dreadful, in connection with *Kristallnacht,* but does not indicate the positive exceptions specifically and by name.

You look in vain for Bonhoeffer's now famous saying, "Only he who cries out for the Jews may sing Gregorian chant." Over against the horrors that baffle description Goldhagen might for fairness have set the praiseworthy exceptions of humaneness, in order to indicate what was possible even in a rotten terrorist state. He would also have increased his credibility if he had made clear to the reader that humanitarian acts of assistance by individuals and by whole groups could only succeed in the underground — and therefore never had the chance to be documented for posterity.

Beyond doubt, the churches failed. The causes of their failure remain a secret from the sociologist Goldhagen, who is no theologian. Otherwise he would not have failed to notice that at least the Confessing Church — in its several theological camps during the first years of the Third Reich, during many speeches, memoranda, hot discussions and synods — was ever more deeply trapped in its theological anti-Judaism. And after November, 1938 they were paralyzed by the terror which they more and more felt directly. When the trains began to roll to the gas chambers in 1941, any outcry, any intervention came too late.

After the erring and confused speeches between 1933 and 1937, even the alert personalities of the church communicated a disconcerting, shocking and paralyzing silence. But to derive from this a generalization about "inactivity" and total passivity in the churches is only frivolous. Goldhagen turns the church deliberately into a devilishly active institution, which is complicit in applauding the burning of the synagogues and threw more oil on the fire. This demonizing of the entire German people, which is transferred to the churches with the same stroke of a pen, does not deserve even an historical explication. It undermines in any case the claim of Goldhagen to have contributed something new. The only new thing in his book is not the documentation but the sweeping interpretation which subordinates itself to the propagandistic thesis about German "eliminationist antisemitism," enunciated in long passages.

New is also the contradiction, which will be a trap for him. On one side is his opinion that every perpetrator is personally responsible for what he saw or didn't wish to see, for what he did or failed to do, for what he said or kept still about. On the other, every German is genetically condemned, so to say, to be an "eliminationist antisemite." What is this? Is the German a free, autonomous citizen who can make morally clean decisions? Then he should be hauled to account and penalized. Or is he a slave and sacrifice of the destructive energy within him? Then he is home free, because determined by fate. From this further questions arise: What about all of the Jews who for centuries considered themselves German of the Germans and Prussian? Does a German lose his satanic German nature in the moment he becomes a victim of an ideology of annihilation? The same question arises concerning German political prisoners in the concentration camps, named and written about in many accounts as courageous opponents, who with their limited means and perceptions helped Jews, hid them, acquired passes, assisted with ration cards, sat in the worship services beside those wearing the star of David, and prepared memoranda or released them prior to some action.

For their intercession for Jews, theologians such as the Hesse brothers of Wuppertal and vicars Ernst Tillich and Werner Koch of Berlin paid with long years in the concentration camp. The mistreatment of pastors as well as repressive measures against members of the Confessing Church negate Goldhagen's ignorant statement that "the churches retained a large measure of their institutional independence" (p. 438). This statement is only true of the churches and parishes which either bowed to the state or willy-nilly obeyed the instruction of the state not to mix in political matters.

When all is said and done, Christian martyrs for the Jews were only a few. But precisely these few are entitled to be mentioned. They earned an answer to the question why, and on what basis and from what motives, they behaved in this way and not otherwise; and what detours and blind alleys they left behind them until they reached that point. Dietrich Bonhoeffer is mentioned only once by Goldhagen; withheld from the reader is any indication as to who he was, what his own pilgrim's progress was until he ended on the gallows with other conspirators — not least for the sake of resistance to the elimination of the Jews. Since Bonhoeffer has become in the USA such a model person of German Protestantism, it is all the more difficult to understand Goldhagen's airbrushing of this martyr. Such historical facts obviously stand in the way of Goldhagen's monolithic thesis about the eliminationist antisemitism of all Germans.

To point to people who at risk of their lives resisted the bestiality of an antisemitism aimed at annihilation can and should in no sense relativize the horror of the Holocaust. But it shows what was possible and what in the future may be possible, if people in Germany, in Europe, and throughout the world want to prepare themselves against the first steps.

Scholars Answer Goldhagen

· *Chapter 9* ·

Daniel Goldhagen and the "Straw Man": A Contemporary Tale of Selective Interpretation

Herbert Hirsch

· 9 ·

Daniel Goldhagen and the "Straw Man": A Contemporary Tale of Selective Interpretation

Herbert Hirsch

Introduction

Hitler's Willing Executioners by Daniel Jonah Goldhagen has become a publishing sensation, almost a media event. The book has been reviewed in major publications, discussed at the U.S. Holocaust Museum and on C-Span, and is even sold in airport bookstores. Like a contemporary rock star or politician, the author appears on talk shows and has become an academic super star. Not bad for a scholarly book on a depressing topic!

In a very real sense, the hoopla surrounding Goldhagen and his book are part of the atmosphere of hype that appears to have become the measure of significance in the declining years of the twentieth century. Content becomes much less central than celebration. In the celebratory excess, sober discussion and evaluation are often lost. In this essay I intend to demonstrate how *Hitler's Willing Executioners* is a much less momentous book than we have been led to believe.

There is a great deal to admire in Goldhagen's book: a prodigious amount of research; in-depth scholarly acquaintance with the events; a willingness to lay down a challenge to previous interpretations of The Holocaust. In spite of its virtues, not the least of which is bringing the story of The Holocaust to a wider audience, it is, in many ways, an unfortunate book. It takes a fascinating, dramatic and historically important event and renders it obscure by draining the life out of the account and oversimplifying complex events.

Goldhagen's Basic Argument

Goldhagen's basic argument is not difficult to comprehend or summarize. Essentially, he argues that "ordinary Germans" (p. 3) willingly participated in the killing of the European Jews and they did so because they were motivated by antisemitism. Not only is this not a particularly startling thesis, although Goldhagen's publisher calls the book a "Work of the utmost originality and importance — as authoritative as it is explosive — that radically transforms our understanding of the Holocaust and of Germany during the Nazi period," but it is, as I will eventually demonstrate, oversimplified. It is not that Goldhagen has come up with a new interpretation, nor that he has discredited, at least not successfully, older interpretations. What he does is construct, or reconstruct, the previous theoretical arguments in such a fashion as to render them unrecognizable. Goldhagen has created his own version of what previous scholars attempted to say, and, in so doing, used a very old academic trick to inflate his own work.

This is an old tactic. You create a version of previous work that is not accurate, in essence creating the old "straw man," and then proceed to show how your research and interpretation not only improves on that previous work, but invalidates it as well. A very nice formula for enhancing one's academic reputation. Take an argument, interpret it in such a fashion as to make it sound almost ridiculous, and then demonstrate how your own version of events, which is bound to sound more intelligent, rational and convincing, is preferable. How Goldhagen does this is interesting. He begins by placing the Holocaust into a historical context of his own construction.

Goldhagen's Historical Context of Uniqueness

According to Goldhagen, the descent into Nazism marked the "departure" of the Germans "from the community of 'civilized peoples'" (p. 4). Without pausing to ponder the assumption of "civilization," and how Goldhagen wishes to define that elusive term, this "departure" — in Goldhagen's view — is unique. One does not need to be much of a cynic to wonder how civilized this community is or has been?

While the Holocaust was an event of great importance and great cruelty, it is not the only historical example in which one people have inflicted terrible inhumanity, suffering, and extermination on another. That is not to say that it is not important or uniquely important, nor is it to argue that there are not unique aspects to the Holocaust as there are to any historical event. It is to wonder why Goldhagen only exiles the Germans from the "civilized" community? Does this mean, for example, that previous large scale atrocities did not qualify as genocide or at least were not as horrific as what the Germans did to the European Jews. Does this interpretation mean, to pick just two concrete illustrations, that the massacres of the indigenous peoples of the Americas did not mark the departure of the Anglo-Europeans from this "community of civilized peoples," or that the extermination of the Armenians by the Ottoman Turks in the period 1915 to 1917 likewise did not mean that the perpetrators of that massacre "departed" from civilization? Only the Germans, for some reason, have committed acts heinous enough to banish them from "the community of civilized peoples."

But Goldhagen does not stop there. He also argues that the Holocaust was so unusual that it "defies explanation" (p.5). In his own words:

> "There is no comparable event in the twentieth century, indeed in modern European history. Whatever the remaining debates, every other major event of nineteenth- and twentieth-century German history and political development is, in comparison to the Holocaust, transparently clear in its genesis. Explaining how the Holocaust happened is a daunting task empirically and even more so theoretically, so much so that some have argued, in my view erroneously, that it is 'inexplicable.' The theoretical difficulty is shown by its utterly new nature, by the inability of social theory (or what passed for common sense) preceding it to provide a hint not only that it would happen but also that is was even possible. Retrospective theory has not done much better, shedding but modest light in the darkness" (p 5).

Until, of course, along comes Goldhagen to rescue scholars from the academic dark ages into which analysis of the Holocaust has sunk. This paragraph reveals enough about the problems with this book that it could occupy all of my limited time and space. I intend to use it to illustrate some of the major problems.

If, as Goldhagen maintains, the change in German sensibilities "defies explanation," then Goldhagen has either embarked on a fool's errand doomed to failure, or devised the most brilliant analysis yet conceived to explain an event which previously defied explaining. Clearly, he believes the latter since it not only defied explanation, but also had no comparable event in the past, not in "the twentieth century," nor in "modern European history." Goldhagen's achievement, therefore, must be most profound. Indeed, if only the Holocaust is difficult to explain because "every other major event of nineteenth- and twentieth-century German history and political development is, in comparison to the Holocaust, transparently clear in its genesis," then the person who successfully explains the Holocaust must, by implication, be the most brilliant analyst to come along. Even more so, since "explaining how the Holocaust happened is a daunting task:" not only is it daunting "empirically," but "theoretically" as well.

I confess to some puzzlement with this statement because I am at a loss to understand how one is able to explain something empirically without recourse to theory, or theoretically without trying to ascertain whether it bears any relationship to the actual play of events in the real world — which is what I assume Goldhagen implies by empirical. Since the Holocaust is so "new," and previous theory so inadequate, *Hitler's Willing Executioners* is, perforce, the self-proclaimed final word on why the Germans turned deadly.

There is no small degree of hubris in Goldhagen's rendition of where his work fits into the canon of historical literature. Are his claims justified?

Actually, this paragraph is typical of the kind of "overwriting" and self glorification that typifies this book. By inflating his own contribution, and underestimating and incorrectly presenting that of previous scholars, Goldhagen engages in a masterful job of self-promotion. In fact, if we take seriously in any way the paragraph quoted above, he claims to have explained what was previously "inexplicable."

How Goldhagen manages this difficult task is interesting. He begins with the contention, as he calls it, that in order to understand how the Germans became a nation of killers, one's "analysis must be embedded in an understanding of German society before and during the Nazi period, particularly of the political culture that produced the perpetrators and their actions" (p. 7). This is hardly a unique insight, since political science has been analyzing political culture and its impact on politics for at least thirty years — certainly since the publication of the pioneering work by Almond and Verba (1965).

But Goldhagen does not mean political culture in the sense that the term has developed. He is referring to a very specific political, or racial ideology: antisemitism. Antisemitism became, according to Goldhagen, the dominant ideology of the German political culture and

"Germans' antisemitic beliefs about Jews were the central causal agent of the Holocaust. They were the central causal agent not only of Hitler's decision to annihilate European Jewry (which is accepted by many) but also of the perpetrator's willingness to kill and brutalize Jews." (p. 9)

Again, this is not a unique interpretation. What is different is that Goldhagen argues that antisemitism was the central causal agent, but, in doing so he ignores the basic insight derived from studying political culture: that ideologies do not develop in a vacuum. In order to understand how antisemitism functioned to motivate Germans to kill and brutalize Jews, one must understand how antisemitism developed and became the prime motivating agent. How, in short, was it elevated to the central tenet of the political culture and how was it manipulated by people in positions of influence and used to motivate atrocity?

As he proceeds with his analysis, Goldhagen conveniently ignores his own presentation concerning the importance of political culture by arguing that, in order for the extermination of the Jews to take place, "four principle things were necessary:

1. The Nazis — that is the leadership, specifically Hitler -had to decide to undertake the extermination.
2. They had to gain control over the Jews, namely over the territory in which they resided.
3. They had to organize the extermination and devote to it sufficient resources.
4. They had to induce a large number of people to carry out the killings" (p. 9).

Obviously, these were necessary conditions before the exterminations could take place, but they are hardly unique to Goldhagen. Hilberg's (1985) analysis was similar: he outlined a step by step progression from expropriation, to concentration, to deportation to extermination. Yet Goldhagen claims not only that The Holocaust was unique, but that his interpretation of it is unique. This is a vastly over-inflated claim, not even remotely true: many others have argued that antisemitism played a central, if not *the* central, role in the Nazi actions (e.g., Poliakov, 1971; Mosse, 1975 and 1978; Isaac, 1965; and Rubenstein, 1988). Goldhagen attempts to substantiate his claim that his interpretation is original by constructing his own version of what he calls "conjectured explanations" (p. 11).

Scholars Answer Goldhagen

Goldhagen's View of the Holocaust Literature

These previous explanations are, I suppose, "conjectured," because they are not "true," while Goldhagen's is not conjectured and therefore the only "true" explanation. It must be comfortable to live with such certitude in a discipline such as history, where all explanations — because of the complexity of the subject matter and the unpredictability of human behavior and motivations — are really hypotheses or suggestions (Hirsch, 1995, pp. 16-36). Goldhagen enumerates five explanations which he asserts were accepted before he came along to set the matter straight.

First, what he refers to as the argument for "external compulsion" — namely that the perpetrators were forced to kill Jews... that they were threatened by punishment and had no choice but to follow orders (p. 11).

"A second explanation conceives of the perpetrators as having been blind followers of orders...that this blindness was the result of Hitler's charisma, as well as the fact that there is a general tendency among humans to obey authority".

Third, that the perpetrators were subject to "tremendous social psychological pressure, placed upon each by his comrades and/or by the expectations that accompany the institutional roles that individuals occupy" (p. 12).

Fourth, that the perpetrators were "petty bureaucrats, or soulless technocrats, who pursued their self-interest or their technocratic goals and tasks with callous disregard for the victims" (p. 12), ...that they were advancing their careers.

Fifth, "... because the tasks were so fragmented, the perpetrators could not understand what the real nature of their action was; they could not comprehend that their small assignments were actually part of a global extermination program" (p. 12).

Goldhagen then notes that the "explanations can be reconceptualized in terms of their accounts of the actors' capacity for volition: The first explanation (namely coercion) says that the killers could not say 'no.' The second explanation (obedience) and the third (situational pressure) maintain that Germans were psychologically incapable of saying 'no.' The fourth explanation (self-interest) contends that Germans had sufficient personal incentives to kill in order not to want to say 'no.' The fifth explanation (bureaucratic myopia) claims that it never even occurred to the perpetrators that they were engaged in an activity that might make them responsible for saying 'no'" (pp. 12-13). Goldhagen contends that these all sound plausible and some even contain a modicum of truth, but what is wrong is that "each suffers from particular defects... they share a number of dubious *common* assumptions and features worth mentioning...." (p. 13). And here Goldhagen shows he either does not fully understand these earlier explanations or has interpreted them in such way as to make them sound quite foolish.

Selective Interpretation

The assumptions to which he refers are that the explanations, in his own words, *"assume"* perpetrators had to be motivated to commit acts they would not normally have agreed to undertake. He then notes that these explanations either "ignore, deny, or radically minimize the importance of Nazi and perhaps the perpetrators' ideology, moral values, and conception of the victims, for engendering the perpetrators' willingness to kill" (p. 13). He then states that "they do not conceive of the actors as human agents, as people with wills, but as beings moved solely by external forces or by transhistorical and invariant psychological propensities..." (p. 13). Goldhagen goes on to argue that what he calls the conventional explanations suffer from two additional conceptual failings:

> "they do not sufficiently recognize the extraordinary nature of the deed: the mass killing of people. They *assume* and imply that inducing people to kill human beings is fundamentally no different from getting them to do any other unwanted or distasteful task. Also, none of the conventional explanations deems the *identity* of the victims to have mattered" (p. 13).

Finally, his conclusion is that "Simply put, the perpetrators, having consulted their own convictions and morality and having judged the mass annihilation of the Jews to be right, did not *want* to say 'no'" (p. 14).

There, in short form, is Goldhagen's essential critique of the earlier literature. He then undertakes his own study of some of the perpetrators, concluding that antisemitism was the major motivating factor and returns to what he called the "conventional explanations" after the completion of his study. Here he reiterates the criticisms outlined above and states his contention that they are not only inadequate "empirically" (meaning they do not fit his data), but also inadequate conceptually and theoretically (p. 379).

First, he argues the Germans had a choice, they could have said "no," but they said "yes." While many Germans appear to have participated with gusto in the exterminations, can Goldhagen explain why so few said "no" and so many said "yes" without examining more than the ideology of antisemitism? This question becomes even more central when we look at his selective interpretation of the second explanation.

Here he refers to the studies on obedience. Once again Goldhagen reinterprets the existing literature, especially the work of Milgram (1974) and Kelman and Hamilton (1989), to fit his own needs. He does this by oversimplifying their arguments, accomplishing this oversimplification by actually reconstructing their arguments in such a fashion as to attribute to them arguments they never actually made. Here is Goldhagen's rendition: "The perpetrators, in this view, were blind followers of orders, unwavering servants of authority, and acted because of this moral and psychological imperative to obey" (p. 381).

Curiously, after arguing that Germans were antisemitic and that most of the German people were antisemitic, Goldhagen, in his criticism of the obedience literature, notes that "Germans should not be caricatured; like other peoples, they have regard for authority if they hold it to be legitimate, and for orders that they deem legitimate. They too weigh an order's source and its meaning when deciding if and how to carry it out" (p. 382). Precisely what Milgram and Kelman and Hamilton argue... Goldhagen's rendition of the obedience literature is specious. In fact, Goldhagen appears to know this because he is his own best critic when he states:

> "All 'obedience,' all 'crimes of obedience' (and this refers only to situations in which coercion is not applied of threatened), depend upon the existence of a propitious social and political context, in which the actors deem the authority to issue commands legitimate and the commands themselves not to be gross transgression of sacred values and the overarching moral order" (p. 383).

Yes, and when Goldhagen argues that antisemitism was the primary motivating factor for the perpetrators he provides no inquiry into the social and political factors which allowed it to become so pervasive. It is as though ideologies appeared in a vacuum devoid of any cultural, social or political context.

His construction of the other explanations he deems "conventional" is equally flawed. He ridicules the notion that peer pressure played a role, and argues that because Germans were "indeed *capable* of saying 'no,'" peer pressure was not involved. Of course, this is contrary to the massive sociological and psychological literature on the influence of models on learning and the influence of leaders on behavior (Hirsch, 1971, 1995).

Finally, Goldhagen concludes his critique by noting that

> "Since the conventional explanations ignore the identity of the perpetrators, they assert additionally, by implication, that had, say, the Italian government ordered such a genocide, then — whether because of the alleged universal obedience to authority, the putative overwhelming power of situational pressure, or the hypothesized invariable pursuit of personal interests — ordinary Italians would have slaughtered and brutalized Jewish men, women, and children more or less as the Germans did" (p. 390).

The fact of different responses, Goldhagen argues, falsifies the conventional explanations and justifies his. But the scholars who drew up these "conventional" explanations were hardly as dumb as Goldhagen would have one believe. They never argued that these were universal traits which occurred outside social, political and cultural contexts. Goldhagen's use of terms such as "universal" in talking about obedience, "overwhelming" in discussing pressure, and "invariable" when talking about personal interests, means that Goldhagen has constructed his own interpretation of these earlier arguments and constructed them in such a fashion as to guarantee that they are not applicable, and, in fact, that they sound unbelievably stupid — as in, "How could any reasonable person, let alone a scholar, propose such an explanation?" It is not always so easy to discredit previous scholarly analysis. Goldhagen either intentionally reconstructs these or he does not understand them. I suspect the latter because he concludes:

> "The conceptual inadequacies of the conventional explanations are profound. The conventional explanations do not acknowledge, indeed they deny, the humanity of the perpetrators, namely that they were agents, moral beings capable of making moral choices. They do not acknowledge the 'inhumanity' of the deeds as being anything other than epiphenomenal to the underlying phenomenon to be explained. They do not acknowledge the humanity of the victims, for, according to the conventional explanations, it does not matter that the objects of the perpetra-

tors' actions were people (rather than animals or things), people
with their particular identities" (p. 392).

Goldhagen's construction of Milgram's (1974) conclusions are not
accurate. Milgram's entire argument is based on his contention that people
who blindly obey are in a state of agency. They enter this agentic state
where they have experienced a transformation of morality. Morality as
previously defined, that is as individual responsibility to examine the
impact of one's behavior and how it will affect another person, is replaced by a new cultural and political morality which teaches members
of the society that the way to get the rewards of that society is to obey
orders without asking what the effect of those orders is going of be on
human beings. In arguing thus, Milgram not only places the phenomenon of obedience into a cultural, social, and political context, but he, in
fact, acknowledges the ability to make choices. Similarly with Kelman
and Hamilton (1989) who certainly cannot be accused of ignoring "the
inhumanity of the deeds" when they call their book *Crimes of Obedience*.
If the acts are crimes, this means they are violations of some law, in this
case most often international laws guaranteeing human rights. In fact,
according to their definition, an act of obedience becomes a crime of
obedience "if the actor knows that the order is illegal, or if any reasonable person — particularly someone in the actor's position — 'should
know' that the order is illegal" (p.47). In other words their definition
includes important concepts of individual and collective responsibility,
thereby placing the onus of choice on the individual actor.

In spite of this, Goldhagen conveniently and incorrectly labels these
two, and most other analyses, inadequate. In so doing he creates the
conditions to confirm that, if one accepts his argument and his rendition
of the "conventional" theories, his explanations are so obviously superior
that they emerge as the only plausible alternative. He then materializes
as a path-breaking scholar going forth to battle the previous armies of
ignorance. Actually he is battling a "straw man" built by his own reconstruction of previous scholarly work.

Conclusion

The charge, explicitly made by Goldhagen, that antisemitism was the
major cause for the extermination of the European Jews, and that most
Germans were antisemitic and willingly participated in that extermination, not only oversimplifies complex realities, but betrays a selective

interpretation of the genocide literature.

That Germany was a culture in which antisemitism was the major strand of the dominant ideology, neither I nor most other scholars of genocide have any doubt. That large numbers of Germans participated, sometimes gleefully and without coercion in the extermination and brutality against Jews is not in dispute. What is questionable is Goldhagen's overwhelming dependence on a single causal factor to explain complex historical events and his elevation of his own argument to the point of self-promotion, without acknowledging the contributions made by earlier writers. If one were to read this book one would believe that, with few exceptions, most of the early work on the Holocaust was fatally flawed, and only Goldhagen has the wisdom to redeem the historical study of the extermination of the European Jews.

It is not fanciful to conjecture how Goldhagen's argument might sound if applied to other examples of mass murder or genocide. How, I wonder, would scholars have reacted to the charge that "anti-Armenianism," if there is such a term, was solely responsible for the genocide against the Armenians, or, that anti-Indianism was the reason Anglo-Europeans exterminated so many indigenous people of the Americas? One could go on forever, with anti-Tutsiism responsible for the genocide in Rwanda and anti-Islamism in Bosnia. The picture is clear.

In fact, scholars have reacted to these charges by pointing out that while racist and repressive ideologies were prime motivating factors in many examples of extermination and atrocity, these were part of a series of more complex factors.

In the long run, the most surprising aspect of the Goldhagen phenomenon is that, in spite of these limitations, his very simple thesis is not only given credibility, but elevated him to a sort of academic celebrity. We cannot conclude without asking "Why?"

Is it because people in general and scholars in particular are attracted to simple explanations for complex social, historical, political phenomenon? Perhaps the complexity of human behavior overwhelms our conceptual capabilities. Ambiguity may be more difficult to accept than a single, all encompassing explanation. After all, if the same person can be a devoted husband and father, go off to his job and return in the evening to enjoy the company of his family and friends, how can we assimilate the fact that his job was exterminating large numbers of people? This is the great enigma of human destructiveness. How might the very same person help a child fallen from his or her bicycle in the neighborhood and go off to Vietnam or Auschwitz and commit horrible atrocities? If we can attach to these behaviors a label, such as antisemitism or psycho-pathology, we may then reassure ourselves that we understand why they did it, and perhaps also reassure ourselves even further that we would not. But most of us are, as Primo Levi pointed out (1984, p. 221), "neither infamous nor a hero" but are "typically gray human specimen[s]...." This is the puzzle and the wonder of human behavior.

Unfortunately, there appears to be a vast audience for oversimplification, not only in the general public but among academics as well.

· Chapter 10 ·

Goldhagen's Book and the Right Wing in America

Richard V. Pierard

· *10* ·

Goldhagen's Book and the Right Wing in America

Richard V. Pierard

Other contributors to this symposium have carefully analysed Daniel Jonah Goldhagen's *Hitler's Willing Executioners: Ordinary Germans and the Holocaust,* and there is no need to go over this ground again. This writer shares the opinions of various critics that Goldhagen's book is misleading, the quality of his scholarship is deficient, and it has set back the cause of Jewish-Christian reconciliation. Therefore, this essay will approach the work in a somewhat different manner. It will look at published responses to it by figures on the political right, indicate differences in these, and point out ways in which Goldhagen's arguments were used to reinforce points of view and advance agendas that he had not anticipated or intended.

The amount of literature produced by spokespeople on the right is prodigious, but due to its ephemeral character and oftentimes poor literary quality very little of it ever finds its way into library collections.[1] In addition, most of the writers are preachers, journalists, or political activists, and they do not have the scholarly training or inclination to take on such a massive and intimidating work as Goldhagen's. It is unlikely that most of them were even aware of its existence although it was on the best-seller list and was widely discussed in the media. However, a number of persons did address the book and its point of view, and their positions will be assessed in the following pages.

Moderate Conservatives

Moderate conservatives have no patience with Holocaust denial, and their responses to Goldhagen reflect this. Two examples can be cited to illustrate this point. Writing in the *National Review,* William F. Buckley insisted that the book is "more than merely historically depressing." It is bad enough to be asked to believe that the huge majority of the German people were aware of Hitler's enterprise, but it is "horrifying" to reflect on whether "its equivalent isn't reposing in the minds and hearts of other cultures right now." He then raises the question of the Germans' undifferentiated impulse to slaughter various peoples in Europe ("if an entire population is inflamed with the lust to kill, how much does it matter who the victims are, except to those who wish to come up with a vague schematic handle for justifying an antagonism"), something which Goldhagen sweeps under the carpet in his all-encompassing thesis that ordinary Germans energized by antisemitism were out to destroy all Jews. Buckley also suggests that not only Hitler had the support of the people for his genocidal measures. The same was true with Chairman Mao's Cultural Revolution, the peasant soldiers of Cambodia who killed 1.5 million of their brothers and sisters, the antagonisms of Rwanda and Burundi, and the hatred of Serbs for Bosnian Muslims.

Of course in America "anti-black (and anti-white) material" is published and we are "absolutely fatalistic about, if not acclimated to, episodic violence traceable to race and religion, but it is incomprehensible, if not inconceivable, that the kind of thing we have could develop into genocide." Thus we Americans have "a considerable stake" in hoping that Goldhagen has "committed sociological genocide" in his treatment of the Germans. After all, one "cannot exaggerate the terrible implications of ethnic hostility. But if it is true that almost the entire German population actively contributed to what happened in mid-century, then no minority, anywhere, is safe."[2] In other words, contra Goldhagen, who sees the Holocaust as a one-time event for which all German bear responsibility, Buckley concludes from the book's argumentation that other genocides of the magnitude of the Holocaust have taken place and will occur again in the future. Given our values and tradition, it is unlikely that this would happen here in America. Still, if it is really possible that an entire population could be enlisted willingly in a genocidal enterprise, then even we are not immune from the threat.

The neoconservative Jewish magazine *Commentary*, whose editorial stances and articles generally annoy liberals, published a most incisive critique of *Hitler's Willing Executioners* by Robert S. Wistrich, the noted scholar of modern German and Jewish history at the Hebrew University of Jerusalem. He condemns making antisemitism the sole motivating factor in the Germans' actions as well as the book's angry, polemical style; the endless repetitions of its key points; the tone of scarcely concealed self-congratulation and pointlessly disparaging remarks about previous Holocaust scholarship; the fundamentally a-historical method. Wistrich shows that Goldhagen ignored antisemitism elsewhere in Europe, especially Austria, and essentially overlooked the disastrous impact of the carnage of World War I, the German military defeat, the communist triumph in Russia, and the high level of acceptance which Jews had in German society prior to Hitler's rise to power. Wistrich insists that virtually everything he wrote about the Nazi ideology and demonization of the Jews in the Third Reich is familiar and has been treated far better by a long line of distinguished historians, and that he grossly overestimated the congruence between the latent antisemitism among ordinary Germans and the fanatical racism of Hitler and his minions.

Interestingly, Wistrich suggests that Goldhagen's book, in a curious and probably unintended way, blurred what was truly distinctive about the Holocaust. By diverting attention from the millions destroyed by desk-murderers, SS units, and Wehrmacht soldiers, and focusing on the relatively small numbers killed by police battalions and guards on death marches, he "brings to the fore precisely those features — brutality, sadism, killing for sport — that are not particularly unique to the Holocaust but rather part of the endless catalogue of human cruelty through the ages." The key fact of the Holocaust, namely, that it "represented industrialized killing on a mass scale, ordered by a powerful state in the grip of a mad hatred," somehow gets lost in the mass of detail. Also, Goldhagen's implication that all Germans "are carriers of a unique racist and antisemitic virus" is quite attractive to many readers and that helps explain the book's commercial success. However, his admission that since the war Germans have turned into model democrats and are now "just like us," rather effectively undermines the contention about monocausal guilt.

Nevertheless, in spite of its many deficiencies the book does have value. For one thing, it counters the self-serving view of many Germans that the Holocaust was simply an aberration in German history, carried out by Hitler and the more fanatical elements in the Nazi party and the SS with the help of soulless bureaucrats. In reality, many people openly dissented from specific Nazi policies they disliked but were silent about the treatment of Jews. Ordinary Germans did participate in the slaughter and were not simply coerced. Also, antisemitism did play a crucial role in the Holocaust. Without the power of this tradition Nazism could never have succeeded.[3]

The writers in both conservative publications have drawn attention to the ironies of the book. Although they both obviously dislike the volume, they underscore the point that one can draw conclusions from it that Goldhagen had never intended.

The Holocaust Deniers and Goldhagen's Book

Those on the extreme right, the Holocaust deniers, or as they like to label themselves, "revisionists," were outraged about the book and unanimous in their condemnation. However, their shrill attacks stemmed not so much from a concern about the misconceptions which the volume perpetuated, but rather from their rejection of the historical factualness of the Holocaust and a deep-seated hatred of Jews. This is illustrated quite well by an editorial in *The Barnes Review,* a slick-paper magazine which Willis A. Carto of the Liberty Lobby inaugurated in 1995 after he lost control of the Institute of Historical Review — a denier organization that posed as a scholarly society. It is for all practical purposes the successor to the IHR's *Journal of Historical Review,* which has not appeared since 1994.[4] The opening lines of the editorial is vintage denier rhetoric.

> The Holocaust Industry has vaulted a vile and racist book written by one Daniel Goldhagen to stardom on *The New York Times* best-seller list. Whether one considers this work, *Hitler's Willing Executioners,* an unintentional self-parody of the most irresponsible "Holocaust" literature or a brazen attempt to counter (with sheer chutzpah) the ever-mounting and conclusive evidence against the long-mandatory "6 million" figure, two things are certain:
>
> Alfred Knopf, the once-respected publishing name, has besmirched itself by issuing this work dripping with racist venom against an entire people, and one filled with lies to fire the hatred it incites. Whether one finds this book outrageously vile or unintentionally hilarious — take your pick — it is the product of a twisted mind in a perverse era.[5]

Another example can be found in the denial newsletter which Hans Schmidt, a German-born American citizen living in Pensacola, Florida, publishes out of his home. In 1995 he was arrested in Germany and held in jail for five months on a charge of distributing antisemitic literature.

In his small publication Schmidt addressed an open letter to the Harvard professor congratulating him on the publication of *Hitler's Willing Executioners:*

> It appeared just in time for the yearly Holocaust shindig with which the docile mass of Americans is now being inundated every year. I cannot help but admire the *Oberjuden* and Zionist activists like you for the virtuosity with which you play the "Holocaust-violin," and the neverending story of the forever persecuted (and naturally totally innocent) Jewish people. To do that over and over again takes talents that have been finely tuned for millenia *[sic]* and, naturally a stupid mass of goyim that will always fall for the charade.[6]

The far right critics of Goldhagen claim that the "Holocaust lobby" is doing everything it can to conceal the truth about what happened in World War II and his book is another salvo in the ideological battle for historical accuracy. A writer in Liberty Lobby's organ, *The Spotlight,* laments that telling the truth about unpopular subjects like the Holocaust is more difficult than ever, especially in Europe where laws "prohibit a balanced discussion" of it. Anyone who casts doubts on it is liable to prosecuted for "promoting hate," and "truth is no defense."

> Time is on the side of Goldhagen and others who try to crush Germans under the weight of collective guilt and justify continued huge reparations payments to Israel and "survivors." Those Germans who lived through the war and are aware of the facts were silenced for decades by a world community that kept Germany at arm's length. Now age is taking its toll.

> As the generation that fought the war slowly dies off, its critics may have the opportunity to re-write history as it sees fit. If Goldhagen's work is an example of what future students can expect, scholarship is in trouble, according to the critics of *Hitler's Willing Executioners.*[7]

This article reveals quite well how the deniers have misused the book. It went on to cite some reviews by historians that pointed out flaws in the work and then implied that Goldhagen's errors and faulty interpretations call the Holocaust itself in question. As those who experienced the era and actually knew what went on pass from the scene, people of his ilk will increasingly be able to rewrite history. The Israel lobby sees to it that the expression of any other point of view is forbidden.

The ultra-conservative columnist Joseph Sobran attacked Goldhagen's idea that the Germans are uniquely evil as nothing more than the resuscitation of World War II propaganda. He claimed that some members of the "liberal" Roosevelt administration had developed schemes for the virtual annihilation of Germany, the most notorious of which was the Morgenthau Plan. Since the Germans had started both World Wars, they carried some proclivity that set them apart from the rest of humankind. The problem was not Germany but the modern state, which "has been the most murderous institution known to history." The institution which Enlightenment liberals expected to redeem man in fact unleashed "man's worst tendencies." Not only was Adolf Hitler "the distilled essence of evil," but also Joseph Stalin and Mao Tse-tung. And we ourselves are not exempt. During the war "nice American boys and civilized Englishmen were trained to bomb cities." Like those wearing German uniforms, they did not refuse their orders or examine the policies they were told to implement. Only after the war did the victors blame the losers for the same unquestioning obedience they demanded of their own troops. "The war criminals always turn out to have been on the side that was defeated." In fact, America's "own moral malleability is evident in the way we have swiftly lost our horror at the killing of unborn children. Once the state says it's OK, we accept it as normal.[8]"

Sobran's reductionist response to the Holocaust is a common theme in denial literature. One argues away the significance of the event by spreading the evil all around and blaming it on some intangibility like "original sin" or the "modern state." Thus Goldhagen's dubious effort to place all the responsibility on the inherent bent of Germans to antisemitism is used to trivialize the Holocaust as a whole.

The Barnes Review editor goes even further to say Goldhagen's "claim that all Germans are 'guilty' of this alleged atrocity" is "driving those who make their livings and meet their political goals by keeping the Holocaust myth alive." They utilize the device of blaming an entire people "to retain their stranglehold on the conscience of Western society." What this denier has done is use Goldhagen's view as a device to undermine confidence in the validity of the Holocaust. He turns on its head the criticism made by several responsible reviewers that Goldhagen was essentially taking a racist stance by blaming all Germans for the Holocaust. It is not the deniers but the "Holocaust promoters" who are guilty of racism.[9]

Following this line of relativizing the Holocaust, Glenn Schram, a former professor of political philosophy at Marquette University, rejects Goldhagen's assertion that "the Nazi Party was the most radical political party to gain control of a government in European history (p 85)." Everything considered, the Communist Party of the Soviet Union under Lenin and Stalin was equally radical, if not more so. The Soviet Union killed far more innocent victims than did Nazi Germany, even if one accepts the six million figure as accurate. "If we consider the evil deeds of the Soviet Union collectively, it is not true to say that the Holocaust was the most shocking thing to occur in this most terrible of centuries or throughout the history of Europe." He also points out that the pogrom was an East European, not a German, phenomenon, and many East Europeans joined in killing Jews during the Third Reich, "a fact whose significance Goldhagen unsuccessfully tries to discount." Although not a denier as such, Schram has relativized the Holocaust and then uses it to support his own conservative political agenda. He suggests that America is moving in the same direction as Germany did and therefore the only hope to save the country from plunging into the abyss is a renaissance of orthodox religion.[10]

Dr. Charles Edgar Weber of Tulsa, Oklahoma, one of the most militant and articulate of the deniers, criticized Schram for writing an essay that was much too easy on Goldhagen. He then responded with a long, bitter review of his own, condemning the Harvard professor for writing an "evil book" and for stating that the Holocaust was "the most shocking event of the twentieth century and the most difficult to understand in all of German history" (p. 4). With this claim Goldhagen, "manifests the arrogant, ethnocentric attitudes which are so common in member of his race." Weber goes on to develop the standard denier interpretation of the Nazi era and the Second World War. He blamed Jews and Communists for the war, insisted that Allied (and particularly American) behavior was just as genocidal and racist, and claimed that Jews in Germany were reasonably well off, the reports of Jewish deaths were falsified, and German actions in the camps took place against the background of a desperate war situation. He placed these arguments in the framework of a challenge to Goldhagen's account of the war.[11]

One of the strangest responses to the book was by Bradley R. Smith, a California-based denier who runs an operation known as the Committee on Open Debate on the Holocaust. He has gained considerable notoriety for placing advertisements in university and college newspapers claiming that the Holocaust is a hoax. In his newsletter he asserts that Goldhagen's monograph "contains more than one revisionist subtext." One of these is his challenge to "a key element of the orthodox case for the historicity of the Holocaust: the great secrecy with which Hitler and his followers carried out their extermination of Europe's Jews." Smith contends the "revisionists" have argued all along that "the vaunted secrecy in which the Holocaust was supposedly carried on was a necessary invention of [Raul] Hilberg and other scholars to explain and justify the bizarre absence of documentary evidence." This included evidence of an order or plan to kill the Jews and the engines of death devised to carry out the plan. If Goldhagen is right about the widespread knowledge of the Holocaust in Germany and that tens of millions of "eliminationist" antisemitic German were applauding this, then "why were the most trusted and security-conscious functionaries of the extermination — the men who were allegedly planning and carrying it out — keeping it a secret?"

A second revisionist theme that Smith professes to find in Goldhagen is that of the gas chambers. He points out that in the 600 page book devoted to a study of the Holocaust, Goldhagen mentions them on only four pages. In a footnote on page 521 (note 81) the author remarks that "gassing was really epiphenomenal to the Germans' slaughter of Jews." As Smith puts it, "the gasings were not central, not at the core, if anything rather less important than the pistol and the rifle in the conduct of the Holocaust." The Harvard political scientist has implicitly trashed "the silly claim that the records of the extermination program are missing because the program was 'secret'" and consigned "the once-formidable gas chamber ensembles of Auschwitz, Treblinka, Belzec and the rest to the wan status of epiphenomena."[13]

Smith also maintains that Goldhagen has "relativized" Himmler's guilt in the extermination program by his claim that "ordinary Germans" continued the killings for months after the head of the SS supposedly ordered them stopped. In effect Goldhagen made the Holocaust "on the order of a German national pogrom." Smith concludes that we have here "a version of what happened to the Jews of German-occupied Europe that bypasses or denies the gas chambers, that displaces Hitler and Himmler from their central role, and that moves the key area of investigation to German policy and practices against Jewish civilians in Germany's 'eastern territories.'" Reading Professor Goldhagen's book "makes clear that he's been learning from the revisionists."

Hans Schmidt contends that Goldhagen's thesis runs "counter to the very principles" upon which the German Federal Republic was founded, namely, that the Nazis were a "small gang of criminals who were merely able to capture the minds of ordinary Germans through insidious propaganda." His assertion of the culpability of all Germans for the alleged extermination of the Jews, one that took place in an atmosphere of pervasive antisemitism, "obviously does not coincide with the Bonn claims." The government will not only have to defend all Germans collectively but also abandon the "taboos" that have "hamstrung the Germans since 1945." People will now have to be allowed to question some of the incongruities of the Holocaust.[14]

Conclusion

Although many of the rightist journals have not (or not yet) noticed *Hitler's Willing Executioners,* those that have commented on it are generally quite displeased with the book. The evaluations of the moderate conservatives are in tune with most of the critical response, but the extremists dislike it for very different reasons. Their antisemitism blinds them to the value of serious study of the Holocaust and they regard this as just another product of the "Holocaust lobby." At the same time, however, some writers have wrenched ideas or comments from their contexts and used these for their own purposes.

Since the rightwing extremists will never agree to the validity of this terrible event, scholars will have to remain eternally vigilant to counter their pernicious influence. Unfortunately, because of its faulty thesis Goldhagen's book will not be of much help in this enterprise.

· *Chapter 11* ·

Hype, Hysteria, and Hate the Hun: The Latest Pseudo-Scholarship from Harvard

Jacob Neusner

· 11 ·

Hype, Hysteria, and Hate the Hun: The Latest Pseudo-Scholarship from Harvard

Jacob Neusner

A revised doctoral dissertation accepted for the Ph.D. at Harvard University in the field of political science, this hysterical book, full of pseudo-scholarship and bad arguments, calls into question the scholarly integrity of Harvard's doctorate. For the three named *Doktorväter,* Stanley Hoffmann, Peter Hall, and Sidney Verba, have accepted as a contribution to learning what in fact adds up to little more than a rehash of familiar anti-German prejudices, dressed up with a year of archival research on some special cases and problems. The work makes a classic error, by treating examples as proof of something beyond themselves.

Goldhagen has once more documented the well-known fact that Nazism was wildly popular in National Socialist Germany. Who has doubted it for the last five decades? But then he has asked the world to conclude that Germany as a nation, through the whole of its history, practiced crypto-Nazism; Germany is singled out as uniquely antisemite and possessed of an "eliminationist," "exterminationist" culture through all eternity. So Goldhagen's cases now are represented as probative of the character of German culture, as though conduct in the National Socialist period flowed naturally and inexorably out of a long history, to which Nazism wrote a mere footnote.

Lest readers suppose I exaggerate the intellectual vulgarity, the sheer bigotry, of the matter, let me turn to specifics. Goldhagen's thesis is: "In the middle ages and the early modern period, without question until the Enlightenment, German society was thoroughly antisemitic," and, consequently, the Holocaust testifies not to the work of a single generation but to the worth of an entire country. Goldhagen never asks whether or not the same statement applies, too, to Russia, Poland, Ukraine, Rumania, Hungary, Austria, and numerous other territories in Europe. But everyone knows that it does.

That is why, formulated in terms of a particular country as sinful beyond all others, such a statement about a particular "race" on the face of it is racist: the condemnation of an entire culture, people, and nation must be treated no differently. Let us not mince words: this is a book nourished by, and meant to provoke, hatred of Germany. Were its topic the Jewish people, its method — give a few cases, in a special situation, to characterize the whole in all times and places — would qualify for out-of-hand rejection as naked antisemitism of a gross and repulsive, intellectually contemptible, order. In my view, anti-Germanism differs in no important way.

Right after the war the German message came through loud and clear: "We knew nothing, we saw nothing, we heard nothing, it was all done in secret." Nobody today entertains that proposition, which was self-serving and deceitful. No one claims that Germany before Hitler knew no antisemitism but that Hitler invented it. Everybody has long recognized that, along with the rest of Europe, important elements in German society — the clergy, the army, the universities for example, among many — maintained bitterly antisemitic attitudes and adopted antisemitism as a philosophy and a program. But the same attitudes flourished everywhere else, and Goldhagen does not even pretend to undertake the work of comparison and contrast that would have rendered his thesis plausible. I have heard survivors of concentration camps debate with greater rationality and reason on whether Auschwitz was "worse" than Treblinka, or Buchenwald than Dachau.

What Goldhagen asks us to believe is that Germany was uniquely antisemitic. Then, to prove his point, he simply ignores the fact that antisemitism was an international political phenomenon, on the one side, and insists that what happened in the National Socialist period can be explained only in continuity with pre-Hitler Germany. That is a considerable claim, and one that, in my view, Goldhagen not only does not, but cannot, substantiate.

For the work of comparison and contrast — German antisemitism in the National Socialist period compared with that prevalent in prior periods in German history, and, more important, German antisemitism contrasted with the antisemitism of other countries simply is not done. But without comparison and contrast, all of Goldhagen's fulminations against German culture — a distinctively-German mode of Jew-hatred — lose all purchase on reality.

That is why I find astonishing that so shoddy and poorly-argued a dissertation should have won for its writer the doctoral degree at Harvard University, a reputable center of learning, where, we surely have reason to expect, rigorous and critical learning, objective argument, above all the recognition that a case or an example on its own proves nothing, supposedly prevail. Essentially what we have is a set of allegations, with episodic evidence to illustrate them. But to allege is not to demonstrate. Only rigorous argument, resting on the formulation also of a counter-argument in a null-hypothesis, can serve.

A single example suffices to show the quality of argument character-istic of the Goldhagen dissertation. I shall now prove, in his way, that Germany was and is less antisemitic than Poland, then and now. #1. When I was student-assistant to Abraham Joshua Heschel, the great theo-logian of Judaism, he told me that when, in the later 1930s, he took the train from Warsaw to Berlin, he always felt a sense of relief upon crossing the border from Poland into Germany. Poland, he said, pursued its antisemitic attitudes and policies far more bitterly and nastily than any-thing he experienced in National Socialist Germany, until he was ex-pelled as a foreign national. And if that does not prove the point, my own experience (#2), wearing a skull cap in an international Roman Catholic religious processional in Warsaw in 1989 does: I found myself jeered, and, unless the bystanders were jeering Cardinal Glemp, walking beside me, I am sure it was because I was marked as a Jew (and a Rabbi!). In many visits to Germany, I never encountered such a thing. Not only so, but (#3) in 1971 the Israeli ambassador to Austria told me that, in the National Socialist period, Austria was much more uniformly antisemitic than Germany. His words echo in my ear even now: "In ev-ery city in Germany, Jews survived, somewhere, somehow, with Chris-tian help. But in Vienna, so far, we have not found a single case of a Jew who survived with gentile help." So here are three stories that prove — in the manner of Goldhagen's interminable, but hardly probative, mass-ing of evidence — that Poland was and is more antisemitic than Ger-many, and so was Austria.

To accept such proof based on examples and random episodes, read-ers have, of course, to suspend not their critical capacities but their very power of reasoned judgment: to take two anecdotes as ample evidence. Those who wish to believe will believe. And so too with Goldhagen, who in a long and much-footnoted dissertation appeals to nothing more than the will to accept as scholarship what is nothing other than an indictment of an entire country and nearly the whole of its population. Nothing in the evidence or argument of this work proves commensurate to its thesis.

Scholars Answer Goldhagen

But much in the work suggests that we have hate-the-Hun-propa-
ganda masquerading as serious scholarship (including some rather murky
writing that invokes commonplaces phrased in impenetrable social scientific jargon). Ordinarily a dissertation is supposed to tell us something
we did not know. But Goldhagen's Harvard dissertation alleges as new
the proposition, "ordinary Germans were animated by antisemitism, by
a particular type of antisemitism that led them to conclude that the Jews
ought to die ... a most significant... source of the perpetrators' actions."
But who can find surprising such a commonplace, and from what history of antisemitism in this century is that observation omitted? Everyone knows that Germany harbored a long history of antisemitism. But
so did France and England, the Austro-Hungarian Empire, Poland, Russia, and Romania.

It is a commonplace that German troops were welcomed by East
European Jews as friends and liberators from the much more virulent
and dangerous antisemitism of the collapsing Czarist regime (not to mention that which was to come under the Communists!). Everybody knows
that German Jews fought and gave their lives for Germany; the pictures
of German troops observing the Day of Atonement during the siege of
Strassburg in the Franco-Prussian War in 1870 are widely circulated
(among many). While German Jews' love of German culture may have
been unrequited, it also calls into question the notion that that culture at
its foundations was pervasively and incurably and blatantly antisemitic.
Matters were simply more complicated. But here German culture is
represented as uniquely and incorrigibly and inexorably antisemitic.
Does Goldhagen deny that all of Europe at the same time competed
for honors in the Olympics of Jew-hatred? On which page? Germany is further alleged to have been characterized only or mainly by
antisemitism, which is a gross misrepresentation of a complex and
rich political culture.

Let me (as a Harvard alumnus, class of 1954) show what I think
takes place in this book by giving another case of the same mode of
argument by appeal to a handful of examples — but now having to do
with the standards of excellence demanded at Harvard for a doctoral
dissertation. Ought we not to argue that the very corrupt character of
intellectual life at Harvard University defines the precondition for the
acceptance of such remarkably overblown rhetoric for a doctoral degree?
Should we not speculate — with a suitable array of episodic examples to
prove our case — that an institution full of ambitious, bitter, prestige-
hungry, headline-hunting careerist, academic entrepreneurs alone can

account for such a travesty of learning? Here is a Harvard professor and the Harvard-educated son of a Harvard professor — the very chosen, the elect, the prince of the realm: does he not reveal the quality of the entire aristocracy of scholarship that Harvard tells us it supplies to the USA? No, I do not think any reasonable person can agree that he does. But were we to mount such an argument and conduct such a speculation, then we should replicate the mode of argumentation that fills and disgraces the pages of this work. That is, lots of cases, but no comparison with the quality of work in Political Science at Chicago or Berkeley or Cologne or Frankfurt! So much for bad argument.

But when we come to logic, Goldhagen's case proves still worse. For he maintains that, since the Germans in the National Socialist period perpetrated such monstrous deeds, as Goldbagen says, "its [the Holocaust's] commission was possible...because Germans had already been changed." *Post hoc, ergo propter hoc!* Because one event follows another, the earlier has caused the later. Goldbagen's very formulation ought to have embarrassed his teachers in elementary logic (if they still teach logic at Harvard). For surely his recapitulation of the simple logical fallacy described in the words, *post hoc, ergo propter hoc,* should have alerted his teachers. Everyone knows that causation is more complex and that explanation demands more nuanced and searching analysis.

Raising an objection on the spot, some august dignitary ought to have asked, "Mr. Goldhagen, would you not agree with me that your argument consists of little more than the discredited, *post hoc, ergo propter hoc?*" That small but telling objection might have served to protect Harvard from the disgrace involved in its bestowing a doctorate on work of such pretension and violent emotion, a work lacking rigorous argument altogether. But then Goldhagen's one-sided and simple-minded characterization of German culture, not in the National Socialist period in particular, but over all time in general, must be set aside as simply lacking in all logical rigor. A generation ago the brilliant historian, Stephen Hackett Fisher, wrote the classic, *Historians' Fallacies,* spelling out the stupidities of poor argument that make a laughing stock of historical scholarship. He owes us now a sequel, on political science.

To exculpate Goldhagen's Harvard teachers, we must suppose that the three *Doktorväter* must have been sleeping on a long summer afternoon, when their young doctoral candidate (perhaps to wake them up, more likely just to impress them) insisted, "We must substantially rethink important aspects of German history," since no serious professor can expect a newcomer to the life of learning, however brazen, to establish himself with his first book as the revolutionary genius to reinvent a field of learning. And, as a matter of fact, the consensus now has established, Harvard's Dr. Goldhagen cannot take his place among the major historians of Germany, with his extreme and impressionistic judgment of pre-National Socialist Germany. For, unless at Harvard (where they exact deference for the opinions of the great professors and their sons) merely making an allegation serves as adequate proof for what is alleged, we must wonder why the responsible professors did not demand systematic and informed evidence and argument for that allegation. The book should contain numerous chapters of analysis of existing data on pre-National Socialist German history and social life, not just a shallow potted resumé of standard textbook knowledge.

Further, we must ask, where is the argument to the contrary, the non-hypothesis to test the hypothesis against contrary data, that any serious social scientist will require as part of the presentation of a solemn dissertation? And enough said to remove the work from the shelves of reputable social science, which prefers testing a hypothesis to merely shouting it long and loud enough to prevail.

Yet another massive failure in a work claiming to describe German culture awaits attention. If, as Goldhagen insists, Germany was permanently poisoned by an indelible heritage of antisemitism, then how to account for the Germany that from 1945 has taken its place as a major power in world culture? Everyone knows that of all the countries that were party to the Holocaust, those most guilty, the Germans, also have most thoroughly addressed the Holocaust, repaired such damage as could be remedied, and undertaken to build for themselves a political culture as free of racism and antisemitism as exists in the world today. No country has done more to learn the lessons of the Holocaust, and none makes a more systematic effort to educate new generations in those lessons.

France has yet to address the complicity of its own government in the Holocaust: its police, not German ones, rounded up the Jews. The Netherlands produced out of its population a higher proportion of Nazi Party members than any country in Europe. Everyone knows that the USSR denied the Jews even the manifest right to claim they had been singled out for special handling. Austria happily calls itself Hitler's first victim, as though no one saw the movies of the wild reception Vienna gave him in the *Anschluss*. In all of Europe, as Judith Miller showed in her *One by One by One,* only Germany has frankly examined its past, expiated its guilt through acts of genuine atonement, and acknowledged its enduring shame, much as we Americans acknowledge the enduring shame of slavery. That is why the new Germany also has built upon granite foundations uncovered in the hidden heritage of the old, a heritage that survived the National Socialist period. After all, Adenauer was a German, but Hitler an Austrian (once more to argue from a single case!). True, the damage done by the National Socialist period to the enduring institutions of the country required long decades for reconstruction. In my experience at Tübingen, Frankfurt, and Göttingen I learned that the universities have not fully recovered. But Germany in a half-century overall has accomplished that reconstruction. It has acknowledged its heritage of shame, but it has removed from its shoulders the burden of guilt for deeds that the current generation did not do and would not repeat and has repudiated in every possible way.

Now how are we to explain that fact — which even Goldhagen acknowledges, if grudgingly, in a sentence or so? For if Germany were as Goldhagen wishes us to think it was, irremediably, irrevocably tainted at the very roots of its culture and politics, then whence the sources for regeneration and renewal that, manifestly, have found ample nourishment in the country and its culture from 1945? I do not think we can explain Germany from 1945 onward without uncovering in pre-National Socialist Germany whether in 1848, whether in Weimar — alongside the abundant sources of murderous antisemitism, also sustaining resources for a humane and liberal German political culture. The consensus of learning has concluded that National Socialism competed with other political traditions, vanquished them, and ruined Germany. That seems to me a much more plausible picture than Goldhagen's, which, if adopted, leaves us unable to make sense of today's Germany.

Here too, then, a reputable university doctoral committee would expect to read Goldhagen's well-researched, carefully-reflected-upon discussion of the competing political traditions of a complex society; they would want to press the candidate to account for National Socialist success in other ways, besides the way he has taken, which is to indict a country and its culture in such a manner as to leave inexplicable its entire history beyond the war. If Germany were the reprobate, retrograde culture that Goldhagen says it is, then how are we to explain the character of German youth today? I miss the chapters on that problem in his long discourse. If this were a dissertation in political science, then the problems of analysis of continuity and change would have replaced the (truly depressing) narratives of cases and episodes. Goldhagen appears to have presented his dissertation to the wrong department. But why the department secretary did not send him to the right building no one knows.

Scholars Answer Goldhagen

That is why it is not enough for Goldhagen to present chapters on pre-National Socialist antisemitism. As I said, he has also to tell us about the same antisemitism elsewhere and about the Germany that, while characteristically antisemitic, won the loyalty of its Jewish citizens and saw them reach the highest levels of society, whether Bleichröder with Bismarck, or Warburg and Rathenau in Weimar. Goldhagen has taken a complex country and represented it in a simple and one-sided way. That is why he cannot explain what happened before and after National Socialist times and why to make his case he must ignore what was happening in that same period in other countries.

In 1920 few predicted what would happen two decades later, and those who did — the visionary Zionist, Jabotinsky, for instance — warned of mass murders not in Germany but in Poland. The country he wanted to evacuate first was not Germany but Poland. National Socialism drew upon one deep source of European culture; antisemitism was general and international, not particular to Germany. The success of National Socialism — so historians except Goldhagen concur — marked a special situation and not the inevitable outcome of the general traits of German, and only German, culture. And that special situation was indeed brought about by a particular concatenation of events and personalities that brought the Nazis to power in Germany. Then they did turn the entire enterprise of the country to their purposes, staining the future history of the country — but only in that measure that future generations would affirm and continue Nazism. But they have condemned and outlawed it.

To treat Germany as the sole venue for "eliminationist antisemitism" requires us to ignore the rest of Europe, on the one side, and to dismiss as an important basis for explaining what happened the actualities of the National Socialists and their history from World War I onward — a special case, to be explained within the framework of its time and place, not a general symptom of the moral evil of an entire society and its history into remote times. In this context, we must wonder, what of the systematic destruction of Judaism by the Communists in exactly the same time? For while they preserved the Orthodox Church to serve their purposes, they rooted out the practice of Judaism in the USSR as thoroughly as Germany would hunt down and kill Jews. How does anti-Judaism fit into the picture? In my view, it complicates matters, and so is best omitted to make the case Goldhagen wishes to make.

Rehearsing dreadful, but familiar cases of brutality beyond all rational purpose, Goldhagen sets forth as his thesis that "eliminationist antisemitic German political culture ... was the prime mover of both the

Nazi leadership and ordinary Germans in the persecution and extermination of the Jews and therefore was the Holocaust's principal cause." Framed in that way, the thesis emerges as both unexceptionable and also unexceptional; no one can find it surprising. For two generations, now, the argument, "we heard nothing, we knew nothing, we saw nothing," which I heard in Frankfurt in 1953 as a young Oxford student who came to see with his own eyes the people who had done such things. Today's Germans know better.

What goes wrong, then, is that, along the way, the thesis of Germans' broad and enthusiastic complicity in mass murder extends its reach and turns into an indictment of an entire country and its history and culture, as though National Socialism were the inevitable outcome instead of a special situation. It is to that incubus, taking over what is otherwise a perfectly ordinary historical narrative, that I strenuously object. My objection is because the dissertation proves much less than it alleges. It demonstrates that Nazism penetrated into the deepest layers of German life, that many Germans, at some points surely a majority, supported the National Socialists, and that Germany in that time united in support of its leader's program. But the dissertation then does not prove what it sets out to demonstrate, which is the inevitability of the Holocaust in Germany and nowhere else, the peculiar traits of German life and culture rendering Germany the unique and sole venue for such an event. As I said, a dissertation meant to prove that point would have included long and thorough studies aimed at the international comparison of antisemitism, in theory and in practice, in culture and in politics, in all of the countries that adopted that philosophy as a principal medium for social organization and expression, not just Germany.

Why then has so obviously meretricious and shoddy a piece of research gotten for its author not only a Harvard doctorate but also a huge audience? For we have to explain not only the work but also its remarkable reception. Part of the answer derives from the sheer genius of Knopf as a mass-marketer, its power through heavy advertising to secure prominent reviews in prominent bastions of opinion-mongering. But the book gains its notoriety not so much from its medium as from its message. To frame that message, let me cite a saying I heard from my grandmother, who came to the USA at the end of the nineteenth century from Volhynia Province in Belarus. In her homely Jewish language, she would say, "Oifn yenems tuchus iz gut zu schmeisen," that is, it is a pleasure to beat up on someone else's behind. And whose better than Germany's!

The market for this book is comprised by those many people who want simple answers to complex questions, who would rather blame Germany than explain an entire civilization poisoned by Jew-hatred; who would rather explain the Holocaust away as a mere chapter in German culture than explain it in such a way as to account for its unique qualities within the history of humanity. The counterpart, in the USA, represents the South as uniquely racist, when, in fact, racism against blacks marks every region, while the South, for its part, like Germany in its context, today forthrightly confronts and deals with its special heritage of black chattel-slavery, segregation, and economic subordination.

This is a let's-be-beastly-to-the-Boche book, and that explains its commercial success. Without the emotionalism, the sweeping anger, the righteous indignation at the deeds of dreadful people (then, and who knows about now?), this book would have sold its allotted 5,000 copies and gone into oblivion. For it changes no accepted views and establishes no new ones. It lays no claim to art or elegance of expression. Its passion derives from the simple, natural emotions of horror and empathy with the suffering of poor victims. These are then not elevated and deepened but preserved in the form of contempt for such awful, hateful people. But that is not the people who did the deeds and approved them but for the German people — past, present, and then who knows? That forms the book's subtext on those pages on which it is not explicit in the text itself.

Contempt for the Huns, like Jew-hatred, is endemic, if not epidemic, and a work that validates prejudice against an entire culture by the apparatus of scholarship, that appeals to bigotry against a whole people through all of its history by inflammatory language, above all that makes life simple and easy by explaining complicated facts in simple and easy ways — such a work, whether directed against Germany or against the Jewish people will find its audience. Indeed, if so august a body as the American Political Science Association conferred upon a dissertation so riddled with bad arguments and dubious demonstrations of undemonstrable propositions, we must find the reason not in a rational assessment of the quality of work but elsewhere.

And where might that be? Just now, when Britain found itself unhappy with the European Community's handling of the crisis afflicting its cattle industry, the old hate-Jerry prejudice gushed upward, and the Germans once more became "the Boche" and "the Huns," and Prime Minister John Major could claim for himself, if not the mantle of Churchill, then at least the dress of Thatcher. That is why, also, the thoroughly legitimate and honorable project of memorializing the Holocaust and recording what happened in it in works like this shades over into a condemnation not of National Socialist Germany then but of Germany before, then, and always. The Holocaust then finds its explanation in the irrationality that that is, anyhow, how the Germans are. That bigoted judgment once more makes the explanation of radical evil simpler than it ought to be. How satisfying to feel such self-satisfaction — to give thanks that I have not been made like *him*.

When, on Easter, the Passion Narratives resound in the Churches, with "the Jews" identified as the evil actors in the condemnation and murder of Jesus, Christians over the centuries have found difficult the distinction that sets apart for condemnation those people in that generation, then and there, but that treats as unblemished by the ancient deed all later generations of Israel, the Jewish people. That is how, nurtured every day for 2,000 years, antisemitism transformed into a massive, mythic construct the calamitous deeds of a handful of people in a specific place at a determinate time. Anti-Germanism differs in no important way, when the Holocaust is used as a weapon to discredit Germany through all time, instead of the Germany at that time and in that place. That is why, in my view, if the methods and modes of argument that define Goldhagen's book were to produce a comparably-argued and equivalently-documented book about the Jews or about Harvard University the work would not win the audience Goldhagen has gotten for himself — let alone acceptance in fulfillment of the requirements of a doctoral degree and even a dissertation prize.

· *Chapter 12* ·

Simply Put: A Bad Book

Eberhard Jäckel

· 12 ·

Simply Put: A Bad Book

Eberhard Jäckel

The world is unfair, and the world of the media especially so. There appear in America the most outstanding books on German history, and they are scarcely noticed. In the past year alone there appeared Norman M. Naimark's *The Russians in Germany,* one of the best I have read in recent times; besides this a thoroughly masterful diplomatic history of the reunion of 1990, by Philip Zelikow and Condoleezza Rice: *Germany Reunified and Europe Transformed;* both from Harvard University Press — thoroughly researched, full of new insights, exciting to read. They receive a couple good reviews, but inspire no debates such as they have truly earned.

Now there arrives from there — from the University, not from Harvard University Press — a thoroughly inadequate, disappointing dissertation — and the media jungle trembles as though a comet has crashed. I have been asked a dozen times by editors and radio stations what I think of the book by Daniel Jonah Goldhagen. I say without prettying it up: it is not on the upper level of research; it also doesn't deserve the claim to be average; it is simply bad.

I say it with regret. For I remember the author as an intelligent, attractive young man. He visited me often while he was studying the documents in Ludwigsburg. He told me he was preparing a doctoral work on the beginning of the shootings in the Soviet Union. That was a good topic. The murder of the European Jews had begun there. There was a scientific controversary about it (between Alfred Streim and Helmut Krausnick) that should be clarified. We had very intensive discussions. Then his question seemed insufficient to him, and that led him astray.

The book begins full of errors. Goldhagen relates how a captain Hoffmann of Police Battalion 101, which murdered Jews in Poland, disobeyed a superior order. He fails to relate, however, that the story already appears in the book about "ordinary men" by Christopher Browning.

Instead he emphasizes that Hoffmann and the other officers of the battalion were "not S.S. men, but ordinary Germans." The distinction is not only questionable: in this case it is simply false. Hoffmann had been since 1933 a member of the S.S. He was to swear not to steal, not to plunder nor to take away goods without paying. This command offended, so he wrote, his "sense of honor." Goldhagen reads into the letter that this referred to the Poles but not to the Jews. In fact there was nothing of the kind in the command. It reflected Himmler's drawing the line: to remain "decent" while murdering.

As is well known, in response to the question why and how the murder occurred Goldhagen answers *the* Germans have done it — gladly, enthusiastically, and from conviction, convinced by their centuries-old antisemitism. Allegedly they were all antisemitic, Hitler and Himmler as well as Thomas Mann and Karl Barth. Before he begins he announces how daunting that is which he is undertaking; what must be accomplished empirically and theoretically on the micro-, meso- and Macrolevel... and that previously practically everything has been done wrong. In the research, for example, it stands unchallenged that the perpetrators acted under pressure and were punished when they didn't carry out the orders that they were given. But who among the specialists *(Wissenschaftler)* claims that? Goldhagen gives no sources. In truth it has been established for a long time that the so-called crisis command has not been established in a single case. Goldhagen acts as though he was the first to discover that. His book, he says, is that revision.

It is commonly believed that the Germans slaughtered Jews by and large in the gas chambers; only technology made horror on this scale possible. In a footnote he refers (without giving the page) to Raul Hilberg's standard work. But Hilberg specifies the death cases precisely according to the documents and counts 1,300,000 "open-air shootings." Goldhagen seeks to gain attention by arguing against positions that no one has seriously proposed.

In the first section he gives us the history of German antisemitism as a steady enhancement — as he says — from the "eliminationist" to the "exterminationist." That is where research was in the 1950s. At that time it was thought that the source of the murder was to be found in an especially developed antisemitism. That since then Richard S. Levy established a decline of the antisemitic parties between 1903 and 1914; that Donald L. Niewyk (*The Jews in Weimar Germany,* 1980) proved an ebbing of antisemitism about 1928; that Shulamit Volkow demonstrated very differentiated insights into the continuity and discontinuity of German antisemitism since 1878 — all of this is not to be found in Goldhagen. He doesn't even refer to these works. (The customary bibliography is lacking in the book.) Now one can certainly argue about the results of earlier researches. But you have to refute them; you may not silently step around them. For the most part Goldhagen picks out of the literature, most of it old, what agrees with his rhyme.

It is always *the* Germans (*"the Germans"* stands on every page, sometimes eight times). If it's not all of them, it's "the vast majority." They wanted it, and so it came to mass murder. No attempt is made to explain various levels of antisemitism. The great problem that the traditional antisemites always meant the German Jews, while in the Second World War it was the European Jews who were murdered (of them about 2% were German Jews), is accorded not a word. All Germans knew it, they all (all of them) wanted it. One must ask why the project was secret.

If some Germans criticized the transgressions because they feared the recompense, Goldhagen concludes that they were in principle in agreement. Full of hybris, he settles accounts with senior colleagues. Christopher Browning, who anticipated him with his book, is criticized without let up and without reason. Karl Schleunes, who wrote a nuanced book about the preparatory history with the title *The Twisted Road to Auschwitz* is dismissed with the phrase, *"The road to Auschwitz was not twisted"* (p. 425).[1] Raul Hilberg, who asked himself at one point how the German bureaucracy overcame its moral scruples, is instructed that he assumes that the bureaucracy had scruples (p. 385). The case was much simpler: there were no scruples, and therefore there were none to overcome.

Goldhagen's reflections on the Nazi institutions also remain behind the present status of research. Hitler had characterized, so he writes (p. 29), the Jews as damaging to the German people. In fact Hitler argues that they are a danger for mankind; and that is not unimportant if one wants to understand why the murder was for the most part directed against non-German Jews.

Most of the book deals with the Police Battalions and their atrocities. Here, as also in the chapter on the death marches, Goldhagen achieves some penetrating phrases. He wants to avoid the "clinical" style of description, which limits itself to numbers and places. He wants to communicate the horror. In that he is right. That is often neglected. But the chief responsibility of historical research is after all one thing: to show how things hang together. This is neglected by Goldhagen; the function and participation of the Police Battalions remain uncertain.

The basic argument rests of course on the opinion that antisemitism in Germany was more intensive than elsewhere. That this idea is disputed elsewhere, for instance by George L. Mosse, is never mentioned. Comparisons are difficult in any case, since the intensity of antisemitism can hardly be measured. But Goldhagen doesn't even tackle the difficulty. Only at the end (p. 408), he mentions it once. With whom does he draw comparisons? With Danes and Italians! Both cases are carefully explored. The Danes only seem "heroic" to him. He is unfamiliar with Jonathan Steinberg's precise analysis of the Italian refusal. The fact that in October, 1941 a massacre was perpetrated by the Romanians in Odessa very similar to that of Babi Yar in Kiev.

Goldhagen says many times that it is necessary to consider the Germans and their antisemitism before and during the Nazi time from an "anthropological" point of view (p. 45 etc.). With this he exposes his whole purpose. Much can be put under anthropology. It is also a section of biology, which studies the inherited and not the acquired characteristics of people. Out of this came the teaching about races, and also racist antisemitism. Goldhagen comes suspiciously close to a biological collectivism. That is a kind of judgment still found at the local inn. When people want to explain something they say *the* French are like that, much as the antisemites say *the* Jews are their bad luck. Raul Hilberg once related the witticism, how one responded to the other: "Oh yes, the Jews and the bicyclists." The other asks: "Why the bicyclists?" The first says: "Why the Jews?" The witticism brilliantly spotlights the total stupidity of this kind of sweeping judgments.

It is indeed beyond denial that antisemitism was very virulent during the Nazi period. Since the research into the S.S. intelligentsia (in *Die Zeit,* No. 14, 1996) we know that it was much more deeply rooted than previously thought. But that it alone led to a uniquely German mass murder cannot be, because there was antisemitism previously which didn't develop in that way. The way to Auschwitz was not straight. Research is definitely not at an end. In spite of everything it has produced some results which cannot simply be detoured around with a simplistic assertion.

The book by Daniel Goldhagen is little more than a retreat to long out-distanced positions. Worse yet, it is a reversion to the most primitive of all stereotypes. That is really too bad. A young man who seemed to me to be competent has gained public attention, but by sacrificing all scientific standing.[2]

Endnotes

Chapter 1

1. D. Goldhagen, *Hitlers Gewillige Beulen,* translated from American by J. Bos, S. Verschuuren, F. Hille, B. van Laerhoven and J. Liefrink, Antwerpen/Amsterdam: Standaard Uitgeverij/Van Reemst, 1996, 593p. The title is a very literal translation of *Hitler's Willing Executioners.* In his comment in *de Volkskrant* Jan Blokker points out that Hitler's gewillige dienstknechten (i.e. servants) perhaps would have been more suitable "... The precise noun 'Executioner' is encountered once at the end of his argument in a passage wherein he, moreover, distinguishes it from 'helpers' and 'culprits.' Jan Blokker, "Dienstknechten, daders en beulen. Goldhagen klaagt aan als goed voorbereide officier van Justitie," in *de Volkskrant,* May 11, 1996, p. 43. The American subtitle *Ordinary Germans and the Holocaust* is not used in Dutch translation.

2. Excerpts of Goldhagen's book were published before the book's publication in the May 7, 14 and 21, 1996 issues of the popular Flemish weekly *Humo.*

3. The director-general of Uitgeverij De Standaard, Rudy Vanschoonbeek, told us that the decision to translate the book was made in October 1995 on basis of Goldhagen's manuscript before the controversy had erupted. The decision to translate was made after consultation with specialists. The book got translated by a team of five translators and appeared in a first run of 20,000 copies. The publisher managed in this way to offer the book in Dutch before the original English edition would be widely distributed in Belgium and the Netherlands.

4. Lambiek Berends, "Nieuwe 'Historikerstreit' over Hitlers handlangers," in *Het Parool,* (April 20, 1996, p. 4).

5. Willem Beusekamp, "Duitsers in de ban van nieuw boek overjodenhaat," in *de Volkskrant* (May 7,1996, p. I & 6).

6. Peter Glotz, "Duitse volk heeft geen patent op massale volkerenhaat," in *De Volkskrant/ Newsweek* (April 26, 1996).

7. Georgi Verbeeck, "Controversiële benadering. Goldhagen koppelt holocaust los van Duitse en Europese geschiedenis," in *De Standaard* (June 6, 1996, p. 3-4); p. 4.

8. Ibid.

9. Jan Blokker, op. cit.

10. Wim Boevink, "Duitse grootvaders opnieuw collectief beschuldigd," in *Trouw* (April 19, 1996, p. 17).

11. Verbeeck, op. cit., p. 4.

12. H.W. Von der Dunk, "De ophef over 'Goldhagen' slaat nergens op," in *Handelsblad Opinie* (July 27, 1996).

13. Verbeeck, op. cit., p. 4.

14. Bas Blokker, "Geen Duitsers, geen 'Endlösung'," in *NRC Handelsblad Boeken* (May 4, 1996, pp. 1-2), p 2.

15. Johannes Houwink Ten Cate, "Zelfs in volkerenmoord zijn gradaties mogelijk," in *de Volkskrant. Forum* (May 4, 1996, p. 15).

16. Verbeeck, op. cit., p. 3

17. Friso Wielenga, "Rechtlijnig op weg naar onhoudbare conclusies. Daniel Goldhagen en de holocaust," in *Vrij Nederland. Republiek der letteren* (July 13, 1996, p. 63-64); p. 64.

18. Ibid.

19. Ibid.

20. Bas Blokker, op. cit., p. 2.

21. Verbeeck, op. cit., p. 4.

22. Von der Dunk, op. cit.

23. Ibid.

24. Bert van Oosterhout, "Goldhagens Eenzijdige kijk op de holocaust," in *Algemeen Dagblad* (June 15, 1996); p. 9.

25. Wielenga, op. cit., p. 63.

26. Van Oosterhout, op. cit.

27. Marc Reynebeau, "De schuld van het volk. De nieuwe visie op de holocaust," in *Knack* (June, 19, 1996, p. 56-62); p. 58.

28. Ibid., p. 62

29. Wielenga, op. cit., p. 64.

30. Von der Dunk, op. cit.

31. G. Van Den Berghe, *De zot van Rekem en Gott mit uns,* Antwerpen, Hadewijch, 1995, p. 131. Although this is not a review of Goldhagen, the author stated to us that this book can be seen as his answer to Goldhagen.

32. Verbeeck, op. cit., p. 4.

33. Wielenga, op. cit., p. 64.

34. Van Oosterhout, op. cit.
35. Klaas Dijkhuis, "Alle Duitse strafprocessen tegen nazimisdadigers liggen in Amsterdam. Het beeld van overtuigde jodenhaters is niet vol te houden," in *Vrij Nederland* (June 15, 1996, p. 26-27).
36. Wielenga, op. cit., p. 64.
37. Eigen Berichtgeving, "Holocaust-boek zorgt voor opschudding in Duitsland," in *De Morgen* (April 27, 1996, p. 9).
38. Van Oosterhout, op. cit.
39. Von der Dunk, op. cit.
40. Reynebeau, op. cit., p. 61.
41. van den Berghe, op. cit., p. 106.
42. M.S. Arnoni, *Moeder was niet thuis voor haar begrafenis: verslag van een reis door een verloren vaderland Een overlevende van Auschwitz-Birkenau terug in Polen.* Translated from English by D. Veldhuizen, Amsterdam: De Bezige Bij, 1983, p. 306.
43. Oscar Garschagen, "'In Duitsland wordt mijn boek verkeerd uitgelegd'. Golhagen daagt critici uit tegendeel van zijn stellingen te bewuzen," in *de Volkskrant* (May 18, 1996, p. 41). The text is retranslated from Dutch, and does not necessarily reflect Goldhagen's exact words.
44. Verbeeck, op. cit., p. 4.
45. Reynebeau, op. cit., p. 5 7.
46. Wielenga, op. cit. p. 64.
47. Reynebeau, op. cit., p. 57.
48. Wielenga, op. cit., p. 63.
49. Verbeeck, op. cit., p. 4.
50. Y. Bauer, "Forms of Jewish Resistance during the Holocaust," in J. K. Roth & M. Berenbaum, *Holocaust — Religious and Philosophical Implications* (New York, Paragon House, 1989), p. 137-153; p. 142.
51. Winfried Dolderer, "Betwiste Amerikaanse politoloog zwakt holocaust-stellingen af," in *De Standaard* (August 13, 1996, p. 4).
52. Jaap De Berg, "Interesse voor 'de oorlog' typeert domineesland," in *Trouw* (May 18, 1996, p. 19).
53. Wielenga, op. cit., p. 64.
54. Reynebeau, op. cit., p. 62.
55. Dijkhuis, op. cit., p. 26.
56. van den Berghe, op. cit., p. 121.
57. Ibid., p. 128.
58. Von der Dunk, op. cit.
59. Henri Beunders, "Een volk verleid. Hoe toerekeningsvatbaar is een

cultuur van schuld en zorgen?," in *NRC Handelsblad Zaterdags toevoegsel* (May 4, 1996, p. 1-2); p. 2.

60. Wielenga, op. cit., p. 64.
61. Dijkhuis, op. cit., p. 27.
62. Reynebeau, op. cit., p. 5 8.
63. Von der Dunk. op. cit.
64. Jaap Tanja, "'Duitser' staat voor 'dader'," in *Nederlands Israëlitisch Weekblad* (May 3, 1996).
65. A. Margalit & G. Motzkin, "The Uniqueness of the Holocaust," in *Philosophy and Public Affairs* (Winter, 1996), pp. 65-83, p. 81. The authors conceptualize a negative myth not as an event that does not take place or not take place as we know it, but as a caesura, and 'as the point in time and place at which the world of our values has originated' (p. 80).
66. Von der Dunk, op. cit.
67. Wielenga, op. cit., p. 64.
68. Ibid.
69. Bas Blokker, op. cit., p. 2.
70. P. Levi *De verdronkenen en de geredden*. Translated from Italian by F. De Matteis-Vogels, Amsterdam: Meulenhoff, 1991, p. 32.
71. A. Finkielkraut, *Zinloze herinnering. Over Misdrijven tegen de Menselijkheid* Translated from French by G. van den Berghe, Amsterdam: Uitgeverij Contact, 1993, p. 85.
72. Von der Dunk, op. cit.
73. F.L. Meijler, "Een uniek Duits scenario," in *Het Parool* Meningen (May 7, 1996, p. 7).
74. Von der Dunk, op. cit.
75. N. van der Zee, "The Recurrent Myth of 'Dutch Heroism' in the Second World War and Anne Frank as a Symbol," in G. Jan Colijn & Marcia Sachs Littell (eds.), *The Netherlands and Nazi Genocide*, Lewiston: Mellen Press, 1992, pp. 1-14.
76. Von der Dunk, op. cit.
77. Henri Beunders, op. cit., p. 2.
78. Journaille, "Willige beulen," in *Het Parool* (May 9, 1996, p. 1).
79. Willem Breedveld, "Holocaust. Podium," in *Trouw* (May 10, 1996, p. 11).
80. Berends, op. cit.
81. Beunders, op. cit., p. 1.
82. Wielenga, op. cit., p. 64.
83. Von der Dunk, op. cit.

84. Van Oosterhout, op. cit.
85. Von der Dunk, op. cit.
86. Ibid.
87. D. Denby, "Annals of Popular Culture, Buried Alive," *The New Yorker*, July 15, 1996, pp. 48-58. Denby notes that the market does not create virtue: "The market is tawdry, corrupt, and corrupting; it is also exhilarating. In a free society, art and schlock come joined together like ship and barnacle" (p. 57).
88. Denby, op. cit., p. 57.
89. See H.U. Wehler, "Wie ein Stachel im Fleisch," in *Die Zeit* (May 24, 1996, p. 40).

Chapter 2

1. See, for example, K.D. Bracher, *The German Dictatorship* [London: Weldenfold and Nicholson, 1969, p. 253. Nora Levin says the mere announcement of the boycott produced such panic in the non-Jewish industrial circles that Hitler was urged to abandon it — *The Holocaust* (New York; Thomas Y. Crowell Co., 1968, p. 43). Richard Bissell states, "Support for the boycott was less than total: in many areas Germans demonstratively bought from the black-listed businesses. Indeed, one local Nazi Party leader advised subsequently that in the future actions against the Jews must be kept secret: announcing the boycott in advance had only allowed Germans to express their support for it by patronizing Jewish shops on the preceding Thursday and Friday.'" *Life in the Third Reich* (Oxford: Oxford University Press, 1987). See also David Bankier, *The Germans and the Final Solution: Public Opinion Under Nazism* (Oxford: Blackwell, 1992), pp. 68-69.
2. Goldhagen, p. 90.
3. *An American Dilemma*, twentieth anniversary ed, [New York: Harper and Row, 1962].
4. Goldhagen, p. 466.
5. *Ibid.*, p. 467.
6. *Ibid.*, 464.
7. Elsewhere, we are told the number is "enormous" [p. 166], "staggering" [p. 168] and "vast" [p. 171].
8. *Ibid.*, p. 75.
9. *Ibid.*, p. 202.
10. See Nuremberg Trial testimony of Rudolph Hoess as reported in R.

Manvell and H. Fraenkel, *The Incomparable Crime* [New York: G.P. Putnam's Sons, 1967], p. 67.

11. Goldhagen, p. 206.
12. *Ibid.*
13. Goldhagen states, "Since the Hamburg region of Germany" (from which the members of Battalion 101 were drawn) "was overwhelmingly Evangelical [sic] Protestant, so too most of them must have been" p. 209.
14. *Ibid.*, p. 266.
15. *Ibid.*, p. 553.
16. *Ibid.*, p. 266.
17. *Ibid.*, p. 112.
18. *Ibid.*, pp. 428-431
19. *Ibid.*, p. 441.

Chapter 3

1. Thus Gulie Arad concludes that Goldhagen transfers the hackneyed theme of antisemitism to the Germans.
2. Hitler, Adolf, *Sämtliche Aufzeichnungen, 1905-1924,* edited by Eberhard Jäckel (Stuttgart, 1980).
3. A favorite source is the work of Rainer Erb and Werner Bergmann: *Die Nachtseite der Judenemanzipation. Der Widerstand gegen die Integration der Juden in Deutschland* (Berlin, 1989), pp. 174ff, where Johann Gottlieb Fichte is made the chief representative of ideas of annihilation. Central is the statement: "But to give them [the Jews] the rights of citizens, I see no other method than some night to cut off all their heads and replace them with others in which there is not a single Jewish idea." This fictional phantasy is given wings by the imagination of the author and — following after — Goldhagen. Even the propaganda statements, so carefully collected, about sterilization and reducing the Jewish percentage in the population, in no sense justify the conclusion that there was an "annihilistic nationalism" developed early. With very few exceptions these are statements that ring up inflated threats alongside the usual antisemitic reproaches (see p. 193f).
4. Klemens Felden: *Die Übernahme des antisemitischen Stereotyps als soziale Norm durch die bürgerliche Gesellschaft Deutschlands* (1875-1900), typewritten Ph.D. dissertation (Heidelberg, 1963), p. 6. From this (p. 109) there is derived the sweeping claim of a spread

of antisemitism in national liberalism.

5. See Shulamit Volkow: "Zur Kontinuität des Antisemitismus in Deutschland," in *Vierteljahresheft für Zeitgeschichte* (1985).

6. Richard Breitman: *Heinrich Himmler and the Final Solution* (Cambridge MA: Harvard University Press, 1993).

7. See Christopher R. Browning: *Ordinary Men: Reserve Police Battalion 101 and the Final Solution* (New York, 1992).

Chapter 5

1. Mommsen, Hans, "Die Realisierung des Utopischen. Die 'Endlösung der Judenfrage' im Dritten Reich," in *Geschichte und Gesellschaft* (1983), IX, 381-420

2. Bauman, Zygmunt, *Modernity and the Holocaust* (Ithaca NY, 1991)

3. Aly, Götz, *Endlösung* (Hamburg, 1995)

4. Browning, Christopher R., *Fateful Months* (New York, 1985)

5. Kershaw, Ian, *The Nazi Dictatorship* (London, 1985)

6. Hilberg, Raul, *The Destruction of the European Jews* (Chicago, 1961; New York, 1985)

7. Tal, Uriel, *Christians and Jews in Germany* (Ithaca NY & London, 1975)

8. Mosse, George L., *The Crisis of German Ideology* (New York, 1964), and *The Nationalization of the Masses* (New York, 1975)

9. Browning, Christopher R., *Ordinary Men* (New York, 1992)

Chapter 6

1. Daniel Goldhagen, *Hitler's Willing Executioners*, New York 1996, pp. 114-116, also for the quotations below.

2. Christoph Dipper, 'Der Deutsche Widerstand und die Juden', *Geschichte und Gesellschaft* 9 (1983), pp. 349-380; Goldhagen cites a translation: 'The German Resistance and the Jews', *Yad Vashem Studies* 16 (1984), pp. 51-93.

3. Peter Hoffmann, *German Resistance to Hitler*, rev. ed. Cambridge, Massachusetts, London 1989, pp. 15-25.

4. Eberhard Bethge, *Dietrich Bonhoeffer*, Munich 1970, pp. 557-559.

5. Fey von Hassell, *Niemals sich beugen*, Munich, Zurich 1991, 2d ed. p. 32.

6. Ulrich von Hassell, *The von Hassell Diaries 1938-1944*, London 1948, pp. 20, 76, 140, 198, 219, 272; Ulrich von Hassell, *Die*

Hassell-Tagebücher 1938-1944, Berlin 1988, p. 281; Heinz Eduard Tödt, 'Judenverfolgung und Kirchenzerstörung im Spiegel der Hassell-Tagebücher 1938-1944', in Erhard Blum, Christian Macholz und Ekkehard W. Stegemann, *Die Hebräische Bibel und ihre zweifache Nachgeschichte,* Neukirchen-Vluyn 1990, pp. 707-715.

7. *Spiegelbild einer Verschwörung,* Stuttgart 1961, pp. 447-457, 471-474; Peter Hoffmann, *Stauffenberg,* Cambridge, New York, Melbourne 1995, pp. 92, 190, 211-212.

8. *Spiegelbild,* pp. 139-140, 147-156, 199-203, 249-255, 535-536; Veit Osas, *Walküre,* Hamburg 1953, p. 98.

9. *Spiegelbild,* pp. 213-217.

10. Dietrich Bonhoeffer, 'Die Kirche vor der Judenfrage', in Dietrich Bonhoeffer, *Gesammelte Schriften II,* Munich 1959, pp. 45, 48-49. Dipper, *Widerstand,* p. 354 cites Bonhoeffer's acknowledgment of the state's authority without the attached conditions.

11. Bethge, *Bonhoeffer* (German ed.), pp. 359, 369, 379-382; Andrew Chandler, 'The Death of Dietrich Bonhoeffer', *Journal of Ecclesiastical History* 45 (1994), p. 456.

12. Eberhard Bethge, 'Dietrich Bonhoeffer und die Juden' in Ernst Feil und Ilse Tödt, *Konsequenzen,* Munich 1980, pp. 195, 213-214 (n. 18a); Bethge, *Bonhoeffer* (German ed.), pp. 555-559.

13. Christine-Ruth Müller, *Dietrich Bonhoeffers Kampf gegen die nationalsozialistische Verfolgung und Vernichtung der Juden,* Munich 1990, p. 306.

14. Eberhard Bethge, *Dietrich Bonhoeffer* (Engl. ed.), London 1970, p. 613; Müller, pp. 317-320.

15. Goldhagen, p. 115.

16. Dietze's appendix in: *In der Stunde Null,* Tübingen, 1979 146-151; Gerhard Ritter, *Carl Goerdeler und die deutsche Widerstandsbewegung,* Stuttgart 1956, pp. 523-524 n. 71.

17. Goldhagen, p. 115.

18. [Carl Goerdeler], *Unsere Idee,* typescript, Berlin Nov. 1944, Bundesarchiv Koblenz, Nl Goerdeler 26, pp. 10-12; Ritter, pp. 68, 77-78, 430-431, 434-440; Marianne Meyer-Krahmer, *Carl Goerdeler und sein Weg in den Widerstand,* Freiburg im Breisgau 1989, p. 73; Kap. 1 Nr. 122, Kap 10 G Nr. 685 Bd. 1, and *Verhandlungen der Stadtverordneten zu Leipzig 1935,* Band I, 30 Jan. 1935, Stadtarchiv Leipzig; RGBl. I 1933, pp. 222, 399-410.

19. [Carl Goerdeler], 'Das Ziel', *Beck und Goerdeler,* Munich, 1965, pp. 105-107.

20. Bethge, *Bonhoeffer* (German edn), pp. 796, 836-837; H[elmut] Kr[ausnick], 'Goerdeler und die Deportation der Leipziger Juden', *Vierteljahrshefte für Zeitgeschichte* 13 (1965), pp. 338-339.
21. [Carl Goerdeler], *Gedanken eines zum Tode Verurteilten über die deutsche Zukunft*, typescript, [Berlin Sept. 1944], Bundesarchiv Koblenz, Nl Goerdeler 26, p. 25.
22. Stadtarchiv Leipzig Cap. 26A Nr. 39, Kap. 10 G Nr. 685 Bd. 1 and 2. Manfred Unger — 'Die "Endlösung" in Leipzig. Dokumente zur Geschichte der Judenverfolgung 1933-1945', *Zeitschrift für Geschichtswissenschaft* 11 (1963), p. 944 — wrote while head of the Stadtarchiv, suppressing Goerdeler's true position and Haake's denunciations.
23. Ritter, pp. 167-168.
24. A. P. Young, *The 'X' Documents*, London 1974, pp. 45-49, 59, 136, 139, 154-162, 177.
25. Goerdeler, *Gedanken*, pp. 25, 37-38 and *Idee*, pp. 12, 14, 19-22; Ritter, p. 613; *Spiegelbild*, p. 474.
26. Werner Traber to Walter Baum 28 May 1957, IfZ ZS 1797.
27. *Spiegelbild*, pp. 447-457.
28. Hermann Teske, *Die silbernen Spiegel*, Heidelberg 1952, p. 31.
29. Hoffmann, *Stauffenberg*, pp. 114, 133, 151-153, 226.
30. *Spiegelbild*, pp. 199-202.
31. Hoffmann, *Stauffenberg*, pp. 107-110, 146, 197, 226, 232, 236, 243.
32. Hoffmann, *Stauffenberg*, chapter 8.
33. Cf. Willi Graf, *Briefe und Aufzeichnungen*, Frankfurt am Main 1988. *Spiegelbild*, pp. 110, 199-202, 420, 431, 443, 450, 471-474, 501, 520; Osas, p. 98; Theodor Steltzer, *Sechzig Jahre Zeitgenosse*, Munich 1966, p. 147; Bethge, *Bonhoeffer* (Engl. ed.), p. 613; *Trial of the Major War Criminals* before the International Military Tribunal Nuremberg 14 November 1945-1 October 1946, vol. XXXIII, Nuremberg 1949, p. 424; Ivar Anderson, *Diary* 14 Dec. 1942, Kungliga Biblioteket, Stockholm, Ivar Andersons papper L 91; Inge Scholl, *Die weisse Rose*, Frankfurt am Main 1952; *The White Rose*, Munich 1991, p. 60; Hassell (German ed.), pp. 62-63, 67-68, 130, 330; *Spiegelbild*, p. 501; Dr. Theodor Haubauch in his People's Court trial on 17 Jan. 1945, *Volksgerichtshof-Prozesse*, p. 100; Freya von Moltke, Michael Balfour, Julian Frisby, *Helmuth James von Moltke 1907-1945*, Stuttgart [1975], p. 215; Helmuth James von Moltke, *Briefe an Freya 1939-1945*, Munich 1988, pp. 317-319; Hassell

(German ed.), pp. 70, 330; report on Popitz's trial, Princeton University, *A. W. Dulles Papers*, IV g 10 b 57/44 gRs 4 Oct. 1944; Detlef Graf von Schwerin, *"Dann sind's die besten Köpfe, die man henkt"*, Munich, Zurich [1991], p. 426; Ger van Roon, *Wilhelm Staehle*, Munich 1969, p. 88; Hoffmann, *Stauffenberg*, pp. 133, 151, 226; Spiegelbild, pp. 199-202;

34. Dipper, *Der Deutsche Widerstand*, pp. 349, 354.
35. Bethge, *Bonhoeffer* (German edn), pp. 835-836; Hoffmann, *Stauffenberg*, pp. 210-212.
36. Rudolf Fahrner to the author 9 May 1977.
37. *Spiegelbild*, pp. 449-450, 457, 471.

Chapter 9

1. At the same time I was reading Goldhagen's book, I was also reading Stephen Hawking's *A Brief History of Time* (1988). By contrast, Hawking takes an obscure, difficult to understand and highly abstract subject and makes it not only fascinating but intelligible.
2. John Weiss' account, *The Ideology of Death*, also published in 1996, is far superior to Goldhagen's account. Weiss makes no claim that he has discovered the single most influential factor and he places antisemitism in the requisite historical, political, and cultural context.

References (Chapter 9)

Almond, Gabriel A. and Sidney Verba. 1965. *The Civic Culture*. Boston: Little Brown.

Hawking, Stephen. 1988. *A Brief History of Time: From the Big Bang to Black Holes*. New York: Bantam Books.

Hilberg, Raul. 1985. *The Destruction of the European Jews*. 3 vols. New York: Holmes and Meier.

Hirsch, Herbert. 1971. *Poverty and Politicization: Political Socialization in an American Subculture*. New York: The Free Press.

_____ 1995. *Genocide and the Politics of Memory: Studying Death to Preserve Life*. Chapel Hill: The University of North Carolina Press.

Isaac, Jules. 1964. *The Teaching of Contempt: Christian Roots of Anti-Semitism*. New York: Holt, Rinehart and Winston.

Kelman, Herbert C., and V. Lee Hamilton. 1989. *Crimes of Obedience: Toward a Social Psychology of Authority and Responsibility*. New Haven: Yale University Press.

Levi, Primo. 1984. *The Periodic Table.* New York: Summit Books.

Milgram, Stanley. 1974. *Obedience to Authority.* New York: Harper and Row.

Mosse, George. L. 1975. *The Nationalization of the Masses.* New York: Meridian.

_____ 1978. *Toward the Final Solution.* New York: Harper and Row.

Poliakov, Leon. 1971. *The Aryan Myth.* New York. New American Library.

Rubenstein, Richard. 1988. "Luther and the Roots of the Holocaust." In *Persistent Prejudice: Perspectives on Anti-Semitism,* edited by Herbert Hirsch and Jack Spiro, pp. 31-42. Fairfax, Va.: George Mason University Press.

Weiss, John. 1996. *Ideology of Death: Why the Holocaust Happened in Germany.* Chicago: Ivan R. Dee.

Chapter 10

1. One important exception to this generalization is the Wilcox Collection of radical literature housed in the Kansas Collection of the Spencer Research Library at the University of Kansas. I wish to express my gratitude to the library staff for their assistance in making available the materials needed to prepare this essay.

2. William F. Buckley, "Are the Germans Guilty," *National Review,* 48 (May 20, 1996) 79.

3. Robert S. Wistrich, "Helping Hitler," *Commentary* 102 (July 1996), 27-31.

4. The magazine was named after Harry Elmer Barnes, a well-known American historian who had been a defender of Germany's role in World War I and critic of Allied policy during World War II. In his declining years, he became a Holocaust denier. See Deborah Lipstadt, *Denying the Holocaust: The Growing Assault on Truth and Memory* (New York: Free Press, 1993), pp. 67-83.

5. "The Goldhagen Tour de Farce: Racial Guilt," *The Barnes Review* 2 (August 1996), 2.

6. *GANPAC Brief, News and Views by Hans Schmidt,* Nr. 169, June 1996.

7. Andrew Arnold, "Battle of the Books. Truth vs. Propaganda," *The Spotlight,* 22 (Sep, 23, 1996), 18.

8. Joseph Sobran, "The State and Moral Flux," first published in *The Wanderer* (an ultra-rightist Roman Catholic paper), April 25, 1996, and reprinted in the *Christian News* 34 (April 29, 1996), 17. The *Christian News* is a weekly newspaper edited by the Rev. Herman J. Otten, a theologically conservative and politically right-wing Lutheran minister. Because it runs lengthy original articles and photographically reproduces materials with utter abandon from other publications, it is a valuable source of information on the religious far right. Otten himself is a Holocaust denier and freely publishes material espousing that position. For further information see Richard V. Pierard, "American Evangelicals and Holocaust Denial," in *From Prejudice to Destruction: Western Civilization in the Shadow of Auschwitz*, eds. G. Jan Colijn and Marcia Sachs Littell (Münster: Lit Verlag, 1995), pp. 229-32.

9. *The Barnes Review,* August 1996, 2.

10. Glenn Schram, "The Holocaust in Philosophical Perspective," *Christian News*, June 10, 1996, 17-18.

11. *Christian News*, June 12, 1996, 22; July 8, 1996, 17-18. Another denier, Patty T. Brandt of Arcata, California, denounced Goldhagen and his defenders as "Holohoaxers" and declared that many survivors took revenge against Germans in 1945 and then falsely presented themselves as hapless victims in history "without admitting what their Talmudic selfishness has done to provoke the wrath of those who finally retaliate against them." *Christian News*, July 29, 1996, 20.

12. *Smith Report,* May (?) 1996, reprinted in *Christian News*, June 10, 1996, 19. On Smith and CODOH see Lipstadt, *Denying the Holocaust*, pp. 183-208.

13. Charles Edgar Weber takes this point in a slightly different direction by citing denier literature (such as the notorious *Leuchter Report*) to support the view that "evidence has been accumulating against the takes about homicidal gas chambers at Auschwitz." He then refers to Goldhagen's comment on page 523 (note 4) where he calls for more research on mass shootings and then adds "The imbalance of attention devoted to the gas chambers needs to be corrected." *Christian News*, July 8, 1996, 17.

14. *GANPAC Brief,* Nr 169, June 1946.

Chapter 12

1. Professor Jäckel, like the other essayists in this volume, used the American edition. The German edition only became available in August, 1996.
2. This text appeared with editorial changes on 17 May 1996 in *Die Zeit,* No. 21 (1996), and is here used with the author's permission.